Saint-Omer and the British Connection

By Richard Cumpston Jones

With best wishes

Richard Cumpston Jones

ISBN 978-1-470046-736

To

Giselle, Xavier and Fabien

Table of Contents

INTRODUCTION

A very warm welcome to you or '*Bienvenue chez les Ch'tis*' as said in the local dialect and pronounced 'Ssh-Tee'. Whether you are researching a visit or merely indulging in some armchair tourism you will soon discover there is much to see, taste and wonder at here in Saint-Omer; and curiously enough much of it with a British historical slant. Having lived here for a number of years, I truly believe that it is still a relatively unknown and undiscovered jewel in a region that sometimes struggles to promote its very attractive and diverse identity.

Tourism should be fun. So with that jolly thought in mind, I present to you some history, some tales and some folklore attached to this fascinating town as well as some interesting places round about for you to consider seeing. The town of Saint-Omer (Saint as in SANTa Claus and Omer as in oh-MARE) is within easy striking distance of the channel ports and tunnel (Boulogne – Calais – Dunkerque) and lies just 25 miles south of Calais. It is ideally situated for day-trippers but really warrants a stopover.

The town of Saint-Omer and its surrounding area, the Audomarois, has juxtapositioned between allegiances involving the Earls of Flanders, Dukes of Burgundy, Spanish and French Kingdoms only to become finally and definitively French in 1677. The links with British history include that it is the original home of the leading English Jesuit Catholic Boarding School: Stonyhurst College in Lancashire. It was the town in which, some sources claim, lived the executioner appointed by King Henry VIII to dispatch his second wife – Anne Boleyn in 1536. Saint-Omer was more than likely a meeting point for discussions in the planning of the 1605 Gunpowder Plot. It is a town that grew rich because of close trading association with the English wool trade and in more recent times was the GHQ for the British Expeditionary Force under the command of Field Marshal John Denton Pinkstone French 'Earl of Ypres' followed by Field Marshal Douglas Haig between 1914 – 1916. It is also the spiritual home of the Royal Air Force through its direct association with the Royal Flying Corps.

The riches of the town and its environs are many. Saint-Omer boasts a glorious 13th Century Gothic Cathedral of note (now classified as a basilica), a fine Flemish style market square with a bustling weekly Saturday market, an outstanding museum: Musée de l'hôtel Sandelin, an impressive Town Hall, or *Hôtel de Ville*, containing a magnificent 18th century Italianate Theatre, a classical style concert hall with superb acoustics (Saint-Omer is one of the oldest Conservatoires de Musique in France), a library that boasts some of Europe's most precious literary accomplishments, an historical aerodrome and flying club, a race course, beautiful historical Abbey ruins, famous landscaped gardens, walled fortifications designed by the acclaimed military engineer, philosopher and humanist Vauban, waterways and canals, two breweries, fine shops, restaurants and épiceries. Further afield there are ARC International the renowned glass manufacturer, two lasting museums of 'Peace' the WW2 V1 and V2 rocket installations of Blockhaus d'Eperlecques and La Coupole, one of the last gin distilleries in France, as well as the panoramic and peaceful marshes of the Clairmarais [lit. Clear Marshes]. These marshes are home to hundreds of varieties of wildlife and species of bird as well being one of France's largest market gardens. Not to mention several golf courses of note (Host to the Saint Omer Open Championship) and hotels to match all budgets.

So how did it all come about?

Saint-Omer Rulers:	The Morini Tribe
Throne of England/Mercia:	Offa 757 – 796

KEY DATES

639   Audomar ordained 1st Bishop of Thérouanne

662   Audomar, Bertin, Momelin, Bertram start building chapels in what will become Saint-Omer

In seventh century Europe, Christianity was spreading rapidly. It reached Anglo Saxon England due to the travels and preaching of Saint Augustin (d.604) who established his church at Canterbury and so became the first Archbishop of Canterbury. However there were some areas in Northern Europe where Christian conversion needed strengthening and so in 639 AD a monk called Audomar (this his Latin name) was ordained Bishop of Thérouanne. Thérouanne was already an important centre of Christianity and was later to become one of the most influential Catholic incense wafting religious powerhouses in Northern Europe.

Thérouanne [pronounced Tair-whan] today is a rather forgotten market town which lies just 14kms south of Saint-Omer. It was once a major Roman settlement called "Tervanna" and was situated on the axis roads between Boulogne, Arras and Cassel. We will hear more about the importance and fate of this town later on. For now, though, we just need to know that Audomar was ordained its third Bishop and his name is listed amongst the names of the Bishops found in the Ambulatory of the Cathedral de Notre Dame, Saint-Omer.

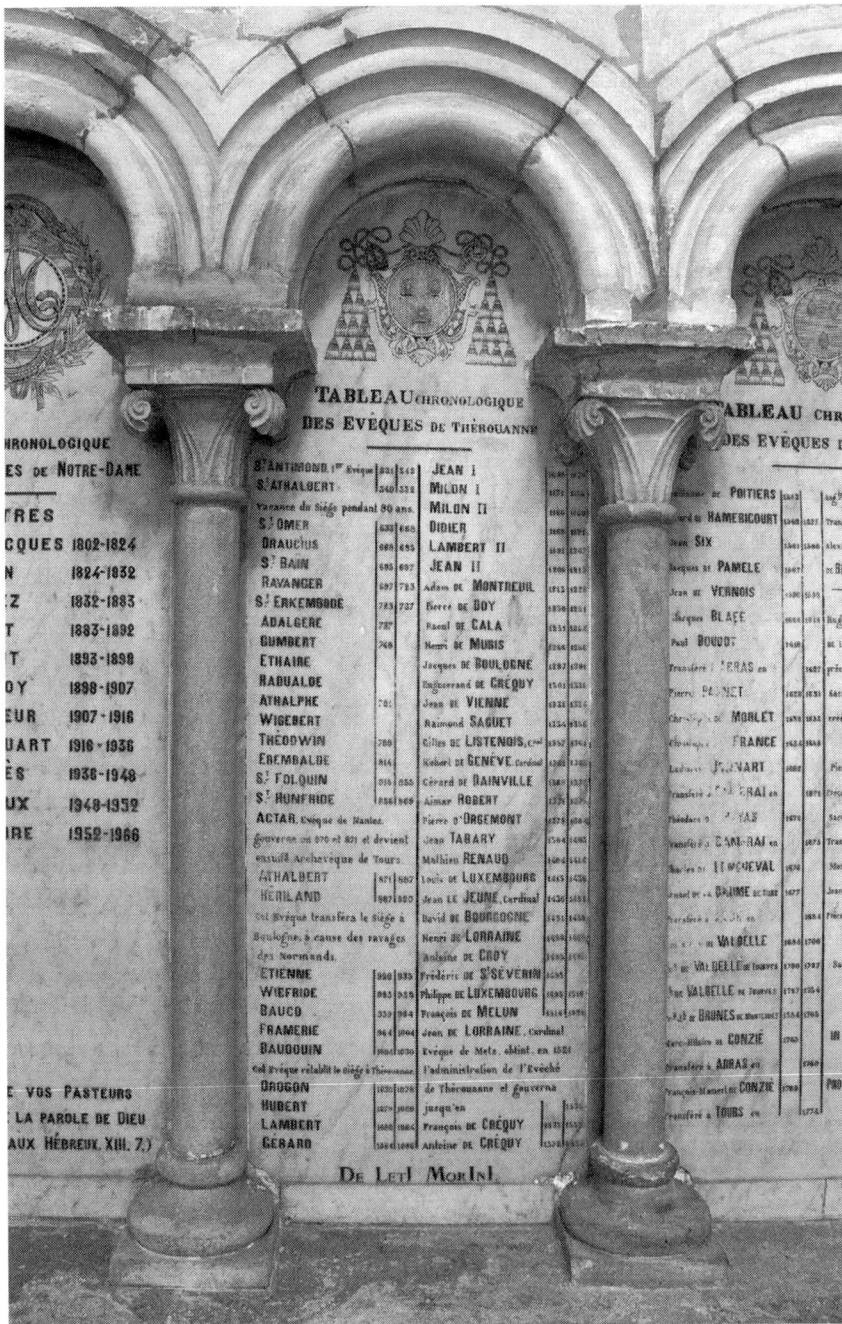

The list of Thérouanne Bishops as seen in the ambulatory of the Cathedral

Bishop, or *l'évêque*, Audomar, might be considered an aristocrat of the times, having had a wealthy and privileged upbringing. He embraced the Christian faith after the death of his mother. Having persuaded his father Friulf to take monastic life, presumably after his tragic loss, they sold all their worldly goods and possessions giving the funds to the poor and entered the famous Benedictine monastery of Luxeuil in Burgundy in 615 AD.

Audomar and his father Friulf being received into the monastery at Luxeuil
© La bibliothèque de Saint-Omer

Meanwhile, in the North, the bishopric of Thérouanne had been 'bishop-less' for 80 years before Audomar's appointment and so it was from Luxeuil that he was sent out to take up his new post and help convert a local tribe of the North: The Morini. The tribal name of Morini continues to this day, the Parish of Saint-Omer is known as the Paroisse St Benoit en Morinie.

However, Audomar did not go alone. He was joined by three other important missionary monks: Bertin, who was later canonised and went on to become the all powerful Abbot of the *Abbaye de Saint Bertin* in Saint-Omer, Momelin (later to become Bishop of Noyon) and Ebertram. Ebertram is also known as Bertrand, Bertram or Bertran. After his stay in the area he became Bishop of Saint-Quentin.

Bertin, Bertram and Momelin being blessed by Audomar © La Bibliothèque de Saint-Omer

One of the Morini that Audomar and his fellow monks helped to convert was a powerful figure called Adroald. This was a significant occurrence because it was he that gave the Bishop and monks land on which to build their churches: The Land of Sithieu. You will see reference to this ancient word 'Sithieu' round about in the town and beyond. Sources suggest that the monks first operated from a monastery which they created just three miles to the north of Saint-Omer in the direction of Dunkerque. This is more than likely to be in the small village called St Momelin. (1)

Be that as it may, the three monks accepted the offer of Sithieu. It must be appreciated that the topography of the area was very different from today on account of the fact that the marshlands have now been cultivated.

Sithieu was the frontier to a marshy estuary that stretched to the sea. These wetlands were interspersed with the odd hillock except to the south and west where the terrain rises steeply and flattens out at its summit creating a plateau which spreads out majestically in a southerly direction towards Hesdin.

Despite what surely can only have been difficult conditions, building began on the monastery of St Peter and St Paul. This was the humble origin of what was destined to become one of the largest religious centres of northern France: the monastic complex of the Abbaye de Saint-Bertin. In the other direction, half a mile away in 662 AD, Audomar set about building a chapel to Our Lady – Notre Dame over what was then a monks' cemetery for those who had resided at St Peter's and St Paul's. The chapel would eventually become the Cathedral, and the area around the 'enclos' and, on a slightly wider circumference, the 'L'Ile de Sithieu.'

The East End and South Transept of the Cathedral © Photo Jonathan Caton

The splendid entrance portal to the South Transept of the Cathedral © Photo Jonathan Caton

It is here that Saint-Omer's most prized monument stands. A 13th Century Gothic Cathedral which has incredulously survived pretty much intact through some of Europe's most destructive periods. It also houses Saint-Omer's sarcophagus which can be seen in the nave. It took centuries to complete in part due to that old chestnut - 'lack of funds' (it was finally completed in 1521) but also because it was burnt almost to the ground in the 12th Century and then rebuilt in the latest style of the day: Gothic.

Saint Omer's empty sarcophagus in the nave © Photo Jonathan Caton

The magnificent Cathedral of Notre-Dame as viewed from Lidl car park
© Photo Jonathan Caton

On the other hand the poor old *Abbaye de Saint-Bertin* was systematically dismantled following the French Revolution of 1789 but is now in part restored to former glory by the creation of a splendid medieval style garden where one can also clearly see the outer walls of the original Abbey and cloisters. This park is ideal for a peaceful stroll or a picnic but be warned the gates are shut promptly by the *Police Municipale* at seven thirty during the summer.

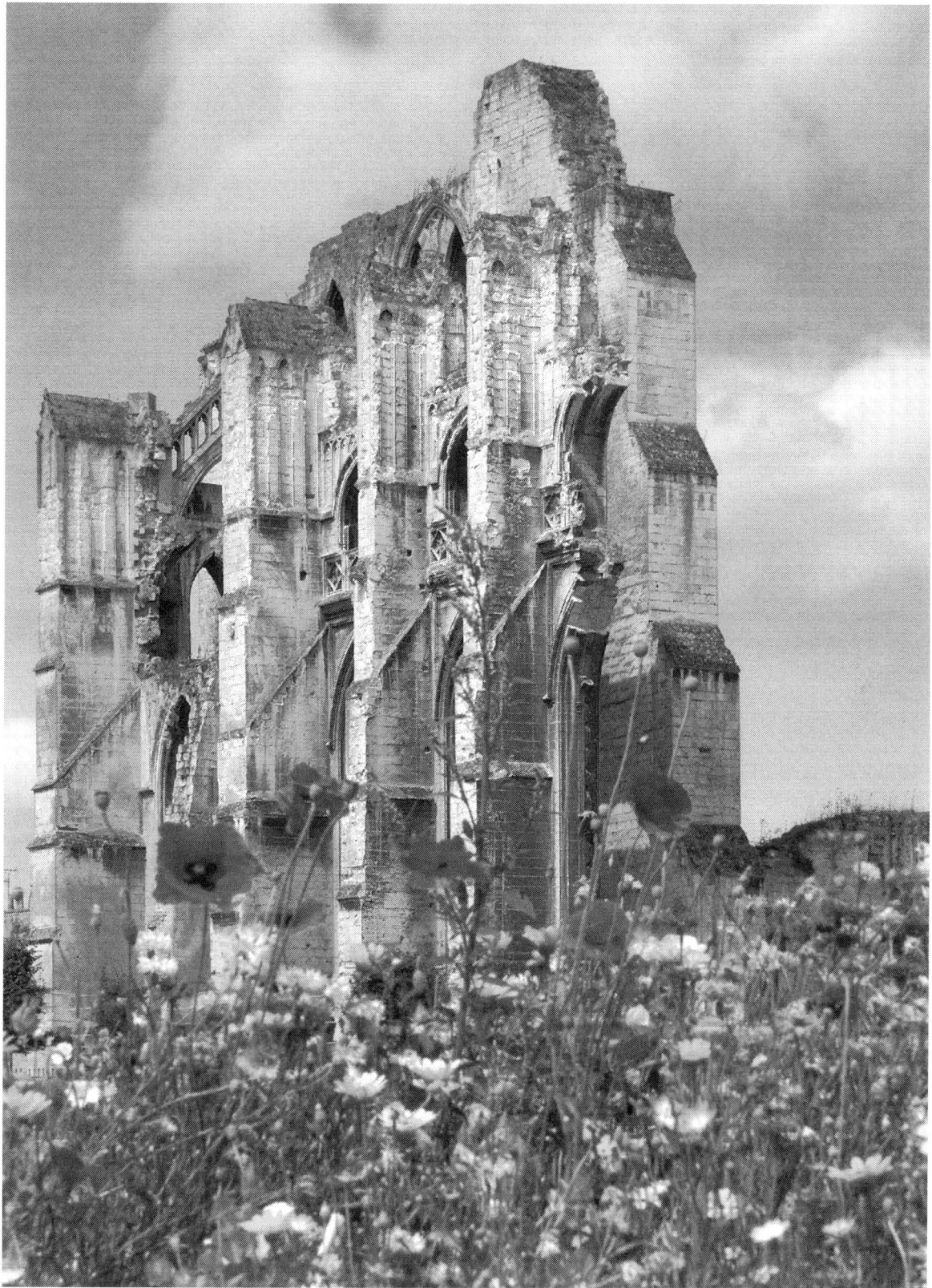

The Ruins of L'Abbaye de Saint-Bertin surrounded by beautiful gardens
© Photo Jonathan Caton

The town quickly flourished around these two thriving religious centres. A route was established, still in use today, between the two churches (the impressive wide cobbled street of *rue Saint-Bertin*) and throughout the ensuing centuries pilgrims came from all over Europe to visit Saint-Omer.

Rue Saint-Bertin - the Pilgrim's Way looking towards the Cathedral
© Photo Jonathan Caton

By this time, the marshlands surrounding the town were being cultivated by the monastic community and to this day, they are one of the largest market gardens in France producing amongst other vegetables approximately 3 million cauliflowers a year! This humble vegetable appears on many a local restaurant's menu and certainly challenges Mark Twain's observation that cauliflowers are nothing more than "cabbage with a college education!" (2).

Part of the 370 hectares of fens known as Les Marais de Clairmarais
© PNR des Caps et Marais d'Opale

Audomar was making a considerable name for himself as we shall see in a tale called 'Les Pieds de Saint-Omer', recounted here by TNH Smith Pearse in his lecture to the Munro Institute of Saint-Omer 'Scenes of Saint Omer' made on the 25th May 1917. There are other versions of this tale which it has to be said have considerable differences but for the purpose of this book I am going to stick with the version retold by Smith Pearse. He says that not far from the Cathedral is a place called 'Les Pieds de Saint-Omer' or 'The Feet of Saint-Omer'. The story goes that Audomar once attended incognito (or so he thought) a trial of a notable local pirate whom he had once converted. During the proceedings, the hearing was interrupted because the crowd had however recognized Audomar and wanted to make a great deal about it. Not wishing this at all, Audomar suddenly 'disappeared' and nothing could be found of him save the imprint of his feet. The pirate was so delighted at having been visited by this holy man during his hour of need, but was doubly so when he and the crowd found only the traces of Audomar's feet imprinted in the ground, so they marked the spot with a pile of stones. There is no further mention as to the pirate's fate; innocent or otherwise!

An important bar was transcended in the 8th Century when the town achieved the status of a collegiate town. In essence this meant that the towns' chapels were elevated to a Church or an Abbey, Chapterhouses and other buildings were added and administered by an Abbot or Provost, Canons and Monks. In terms of the *enclos* this meant the creation of an enclosure comprising seventeen houses, cloisters that were independent from the town, a library, a school, a chapterhouse and most importantly a large *Cave-à-Vin!* All this accessed by a series of five portals. And as to the future – this meant power, wealth and influence.

Looking up towards the north transept of the Cathedral through the
archway of rue de l'Echelle © Photo Jonathan Caton

Saint-Omer, Charlemagne and Offa, King of Mercia and the Anglo Saxons

As the town grew, so did its reputation. Although improbable in terms of the chronology of some of the historical characters, Smith Pearse tells us that by the time of Charles the Great, who was crowned Holy Roman Emperor in 800 A.D., Saint-Omer was evidently a flourishing town, doing considerable work, so much so that he paid it a special visit. Charlemagne found in Saint-Omer so many learned men and students that he was able to send some over to England to convert the island. King Alfred was very anxious to obtain the assistance of French scholars of the day in order to educate his people and he asked Charlemagne to help him.

After the time of Charlemagne (742 – 814 A.D.) his empire was divided up. In his heyday Charlemagne was Emperor of practically all of France and Germany and he held his court at Aix-la-Chapelle. He had three sons, one of whom took Germany, another France and the other Lorraine. Saint-Omer had always been a frontier town on the borders of Lorraine and for a large part of its history it was a key Flemish town, in fact some 700 years of its history are Flemish. (3) It is more likely that Smith Pearse actually meant Offa, King of Mercia (757 – 796) whom Charlemagne treated as an equal, and not King Alfred who came to the throne after Charlemagne's death in 814 A.D.

Neither Saint-Omer nor the Episcopal town of Thérouanne escaped the attention of the Vikings or Normans. Both towns were attacked between 860 and 880 A.D, with varying degrees of success. As terrifying as these raids undoubtedly were, they were never severe enough to threaten the extinction of either settlement. In fact both towns recovered and were the stronger for it. As for the Vikings, some set up home in the area in the town of Guines, 20kms north of Saint-Omer.

Saint-Omer was now in the hands of the Flemish Law Lords and they recognised the value of the town and its rapidly growing power and influence. It was therefore in the interest of these Flemish overlords to protect the town as best they could. This not only meant investing in better defences but also in making sure that the 'right' person was in overall charge of the religious institutions. This was a delicate balancing act and one with which the Church authorities had to take a very active role in satisfying both the wishes of their masters but also seeing to the considerable needs of the people. With this in mind a market place was established near to the one that operates to this day every Saturday morning on *Place Foch* (pronounced Fosh).

The busy and most excellent value Saturday market on Place Foch © Photo Jonathan Caton

Due to the lie of the land on which Saint-Omer sits, the town was relatively easy to defend. The highest point is the *Enclos* and it was here that the Flemish Princes built a balustrade of some 600 metres from earth and wood and fashioned a mound (4) on which in the 10th Century they constructed a castle. Over time this mound was developed and became the site of the town's prison. Today it is a rather fine townhouse.

Saint-Omer, in its history, has always been vulnerable to a sacking and so from this time onwards its fortifications were always under review and at various periods for the next 900 years they were regularly upgraded. The most spectacular of which have to be the fortifications that you can see from the *Jardin Public – boulevard Vauban*. These defensive walls originate from the 16th Century.

Vauban's Defences in the Jardin Public © Photo Jonathan Caton

The 12th Century: Early Trade and Favourable Terms

Saint-Omer Rulers: Counts of Flanders

Throne of England: Stephen (b.1090) k.fr: 1135 – 1154

                                    Henry II (b.1133) k.fr: 1154 – 1189

                                    Richard 1 (b.1157) k.fr: 1189 – 1199

KEY DATES

1127	Charter of Saint-Omer
	Marshlands cultivated further by the creation of 'Wateringues'
1135	onwards – Abbot Suger instrumental in developing the Gothic Style at the Church of St Denis in Paris
1140	Cistercian order sets up in Clairmarais
1152	England by marriage becomes part of the kingdoms of Anjou and Aquitaine
1154	Henry II starts the Plantagenet Dynasty of English Kings
1160's	Canal is built connecting Saint-Omer to river Aa
1164	Thomas Becket seeks refuge in Clairmarais
1175	Metal worker *de HUY* starts his *Pied de Croix de St Bertin* as seen in Musée de l'Hôtel Sandelin
1197	Forces allied to Richard 1 of England and Baudouin IX, Count of Flanders besiege Saint-Omer

The 12th century was very profitable for the town of Saint-Omer. Trade was increasing and the town was bustling with busy merchants. In 1127 further trading strength was brought to the citizens. A local Count of some considerable influence called Guillaume Cliton decided that it would be in the best interest of the traders of Saint-Omer to unite so that they acted under the same business code and benefited from fortuitous terms of trade and tax exemption.

So an official charter was drawn up. It is called the 'Charter for the Town of Saint-Omer'. Cliton was greatly respected by the people of Saint-Omer and, as is often the case in French towns, a street has been named after him.

In the Charter there are twenty five specific points listing trading regularities and details of tax exemption. In it, clauses seven and nine are of particular interest for those living and trading in Saint-Omer at the time:

7 If it should happen that at any time I [Guillaume Cliton, Count of Flanders] should acquire land outside of Flanders, or if a treaty of peace be made between me and my uncle, Henry, King of the English, (Henry I 1068 – 1135) I will cause them to be made free of all toll in the land acquired, or in the whole land of England, or I will make them free of all customs by the terms of such treaty.

9 All who dwell within the walls of Saint-Omer, or who dwell there in the future, I make free from cavagium, i.e., from head-tax, and from suit of court. (5)

This charter coincided with the creation of the Guild of Saint-Omer which went on to become a member of the Flemish Hanse of London.

The Charter of 1127 now in the library of Saint-Omer © Bibliothèque de Saint-Omer

Saint-Omer was very close to the heart of the medieval wool and linen trade. The water from nearby river Lys (as seen on town's names such as Aire-sur-la-Lys) was ideal for the retting or softening of flax (the core product of linen). Also, with its proximity to the port of Gravelines the town was well placed to receive the fine long fibred wool that England exported to great demand. Aside from Saint-Omer this wool was exported to Antwerp and Bruges. Flander's cloth was then sold internationally through the trading centres of Bruges, Paris and Cologne.

During this period the Counts of Flanders in varying degrees continued the monks' efforts of draining the marshes. They organised the landowners into groups known as '*Wateringues*' whose responsibility was to drain them and encourage further cultivation.

During these flourishing times the variety of religious orders increased with the arrival of the Cistercians in 1140. They built an abbey in Clairmarais. Although it is now in ruins (another casualty of the French Revolution in 1789).

The scribes were highly productive and fortunately there are one hundred and thirty surviving books from this monastery you can see at the *Bibliothèque de Saint-Omer*. Aside many religious themes they featured the birds from the surrounding area such as swans, hawks, and partridges and were illustrated in magnificent colour.

It is known that Saint Thomas Becket took refuge here in 1165 whilst fleeing from England during his quarrels with Henry II (6). The story goes that Archbishop Becket arrived a fugitive with a few loyal companions on a filthy night in November 1164 at Oye Plage, a small seaside hamlet close to Dunkerque.

Their intention was to make their way to Abbaye Saint-Bertin in Saint-Omer where Richard of Bosham was waiting for them. However as they approached Saint-Omer word reached them that Henry II had sent an Embassy to France which would be passing via the Abbaye de Saint-Bertin.

This Embassy consisted of some notable English heavyweights: The Archbishop of York, the Bishops of London, Exeter and Worcester, the Earl of Arundel, The Royal Clerks: Richard of Ilchester and John of Oxford, Guy Rufus, Dean of Waltham and the Royal Chamberlain Henry FitzGerold. Obviously not wanting to coincide visits, Becket stayed in hiding at the Cistercian Abbey whilst Henry's Embassy passed through. When they had left, Becket departed from Clairmarais and received a warm welcome from the Abbot of Saint-Bertin - Abbot Godescal. Here Becket was joined by some clerks from Northampton, the Archbishop's Chaplain, Chaplains Gilbert and Scaiman, Robert a canon of Merton, Richard of Salisbury, his cross-bearer Alexander-Llewelyn, the keeper of his seal Master Ernulf and his clerks, Baldwin of Boulogne, the Archdeacon of Norwich, Gunter of Winchester and Theold a canon of St Martin's in Canterbury. All present were there to help plan safe refuge for Becket and create a chance for him to meet with the King of France, Louis VII the Young and Pope Alexander III. The Bishop of Thérouanne at the time was also keen to help Becket. He was a fellow Englishman by birth called Millon II.

The danger to Thomas Becket was considerable. Henry II's Embassy was instructing the king's allies not to harbour this 'fugitive from justice'. A visit was made on Becket's behalf by Bishop Millon II and Abbot Godescal to Philip of Alsace requesting 'safe passage' through his territories. This request was denied and so on returning Millon and Godescal personally escorted Becket through Flanders where he continued his journey to Soissons on a great white horse that Millon had given him.

In the 1160's a major local engineering feat was achieved that would have international trading implications in terms of wealth for the town. A canal was built connecting the town with the river Aa which was also harried and dredged permitting large flat-bottomed trading vessels access from the sea directly into the heart of the town.

The Haut Pont part of the town showing part of the canal built in the 1160's of typically Flemish feel. Held along here is an excellent float festival every July. © Photo Jonathan Caton

Its construction allowed the town's waterways to be developed thus giving merchants more flexibility and capability of dealing with larger loads. Vaulted storage areas were built along the waterside. Some of these can be seen if you walk along *Quai des Salines* or "Quayside of the Salt" works. To this day the street names cannot disguise the commodities or purpose that they once had: *Place de Vainquai* or Wine Quay, *Quai du Commerce* – commercial quay.

Quai des Salines by Paul-Adrien Bouroux (1925)
© Ms 698 Fo 6r Bibliothèque d'Agglomération de Saint-Omer

Due to the fact that no medieval building from this time exists today we have to go to another source to give us some idea of the success and affluence that the town had at this time, and one has to look no further than an amazing piece of metal work which once held the cross of Saint-Bertin and now resides permanently in L'Hôtel Musée Sandelin: Le Pied de Croix de Saint-Bertin. It is attributed to one of Europe's finest metal workers: Godefroy de Huy between 1175 and 1180. It was believed to have been a smaller copy of the one used by Abbot Suger at his Church of St Denis in Paris. Be that as it may – it is one of the north's most treasured possessions. On each corner of the stand are the four evangelists, Mathew, Mark, Luke and John. The Musée de l'hôtel Sandelin is the only place that you can see this in all its splendour in situ – the insurance for this piece is just too great for it to leave the museum.

As we leave the 12th Century we enter a period whereby trade remains strong and Saint-Omer is still a valued prize. In September 1197 troops allied to Count of Flanders Baudouin IX and Richard I the Lionheart of England put siege to the town but their forces gave up after twenty-nine days of resistance. (7)

Saint-Omer Rulers: Counts of Flanders

Throne of England: John 'Lackland' (b.1167) k.fr: 1199 - 1216

Henry III (b.1207) k.fr: 1216 -1272

Edward 1 (b.1239) k.fr: 1272 – 1307

KEY DATES

1204 -1215	John loses control of most of Aquitaine and Normandy
1200's	work starts on architecturally updating L'Abbaye St-Bertin
1214	Saint-Omer besieged by Ferrand of Portugal supported by Salisbury
1214	Battle of Bouvines
1215	John signs the Magna Carta
	Saint-Omer hits peak population of 35 000 people
1228	French forces defeat the Flemish at the Battle of Cassel
1294	Edward 1 creates Staple towns to raise taxes for wars against France

In 1214 Saint-Omer was attacked by the troops under the command of Count Ferrand of Portugal whose army was reinforced by the troops under the command of the 3rd Earl of Salisbury, William Longespée. Saint-Omer withstood the attack and the aggressors withdrew burning the Faubourg area of the town as they went. (8)

The Counts of Flanders were still in overall charge but their 700 year tenancy was slowly coming to an end. They were soldiers and often preferred Crusading to governing their lands back home and they found that ruling from afar was not an easy thing to do and bit by bit they lost their grip on governing Flanders – soon the towns' authorities usurped their positions. As a result there are no real records after the 13th Century for the Counts of Flanders ruling over the town of Saint-Omer. Their hold on Flanders was lessened further by two significant conflicts. The first occurred on Sunday 27th July 1214 at the Battle of Bouvines.

The battle took place in an area between Lille and Tournai (about 100kms east of Saint-Omer) and was a decisive victory for the French.

The French King Philip II Augustus (1165 – 1223) and his forces defeated the combined armies of the then Holy Roman Emperor Otto IV, King John of England, Ferdinand of Portugal – Count of Flanders and Renaud of Dammartin, Count of Boulogne. The French victory boosted France's standing and gave the perception of increased power and influence for the French monarchy. It led to France's overall control of Normandy and forced King John to sign the Magna Carta creating the path to British Common Law. The second was another decisive victory for the French at the Battle of Cassel in 1228. As a result of this victory France gained control of most of Flanders but at the expense of making herself very unpopular with the people of Flanders. This resentment made it easy for the Flemish people to support the English during the forthcoming 100 Years war.

During this period and it is hard to imagine today, Saint-Omer reached its zenith in terms of inhabitants. Thirty-five thousand citizens are recorded to have lived within the fortified walls. Today the total is roughly half that. Quite frankly the thought is quite hideous and the famous French historian Jules Michelet's befitting description of the Middle Ages as "the thousand years without baths" could not sum up the hygiene situation of the masses more aptly! Medieval overcrowding on this scale was common but imagine the problems of sanitation – or rather don't!

Saint-Omer Rulers: Counts of Flanders up to 1369

1369 – 1516 Dukes of Burgundy

Throne of England: Edward II (b.1284) k.fr: 1307 - 1327

Edward III (b.1312) k.fr: 1327 - 1377

Richard II (b.1367) k.fr: 1377 – 1399

KEY DATES

1314   Defeat for Edward III by the Scottish at the Battle of Bannockburn

1314   Saint-Omer is chosen as the first Staple Town

1330   Edward III's eldest son born: Edward the Black Prince

1337   Start of the 100 years war

1337   Troops allied to Edward III besiege Saint-Omer unsuccessfully

1339   Duke of Gloucester commands siege – attempt fails

1340   The Black Death begins to ravage medieval Europe

1340   Edward III defeats French navy at the Battle of Sluys

1340   Battle of Saint-Omer, French victory over the forces loyal to Edward III

1346   Edward III defeats French at Crécy

1360   Treaty of Brétigny between Edward III and John II (The Good) of France

1369   Dukes of Burgundy start their rule of Flanders

1384   Saint-Omer falls into the Burgundian fold after Philip the Bold's marriage to Margaret, heiress of Flanders

Saint-Omer the English Staple Town

Saint-Omer continued to produce in unmitigated concentration, religion and healthcare, the two always seem to go hand in hand. In addition Saint-Omer was continuing to become increasingly rich, thanks to the Wool Trade of Flanders. Wool in the Medieval Ages was the 'oil' of modern times. Kingdoms were lubricated by it and now more than ever Monarch's used this trade as one of the main contributors to their coffers.

Saint-Omer for a number of years was made the first compulsory 'Staple' town for the Wool Trade between Flanders and the Merchants of England in particular London.

What was a 'staple' town? Staples were instigated by Edward 1 of England around 1294 to help fund his war with the French. In layman's terms it meant that all wool had to pass through a series of legitimately appointed towns where it was traded and taxes collected thus generating considerable sums of money not only for the powers that be but also for the merchants themselves. So after much debate in London in the spring of 1314 Saint-Omer was chosen to be the first 'Staple'. It is noted by Eileen Power in her Ford lecture of 1941 on the English Wool trade that much discussion on the topic had taken place at the 'Lion Tavern' in the Mercery (9) particularly by spice merchant Richard de Béthune (Mayor of the Staple) who pressed hard for this decision. Eligibility to partake in this debate was based on the fact that all members were a merchant or a London citizen.

Saint-Omer found favour with the merchants because it enjoyed a rich volume of trade and had easy access to the sea but it also benefited from privileges meted out by the English Crown and already had a long tradition with English trade as we saw with the favourable terms given it by Guillaume Cliton. The staple status shifted around the area going to Antwerp and Bruges on occasion. It was finally presented to Calais in the 1360s where it stayed.

As history tells us monarchs in-waiting wanting to succeed often had to apply a degree of force. And so for this reason came an end to a flourishing period of prosperity - disrupted by what we now refer to as The 100 Years' War.

We have to retrace history back to the Norman conquest of 1066 to understand the reasons why such a war took place. The 100 Years' War was a series of bloody conflicts principally between the English and French which lasted over an exhausting period of 116 years. Their historical description as the 100 Year's war is merely convention. When Anglo -Saxon England was successfully conquered by the Normans it was drawn into the confines of Norman France. As time marched on, England, through several royal marriages became an extension to the Kingdoms of Anjou and Aquitaine in 1154. This was the Plantagenet side. The surname "Plantagenet" to my mind conjures up images of steely riveted and ornately decorated armour, majestic coats-of-arms, knights, heralds, double handed swords, duelling, jousting and banqueting. The word however has a humbler meaning and is taken from a piece of decoration in the head gear worn by Geoffrey of Anjou and his men who used to sport a piece of broom in their hats. This cutting of foliage in French is a 'plante genêt'.

The competing dynasty to the Plantagenet's was the Capetian. They had been ruling much of the other 'half' of France since 987 AD. The Capetians would evolve into the House of Bourbon and from there become the official Royal Household of France which would last right up to the end of the Reformation with the death of Louis-Philippe of the Orleans branch in 1848.

And so it was in this war-mongering century that the Capetian Dynasty redoubled its efforts to rule and control the whole of France. The Plantagenet's had other ideas.

Events exploded when Edward III of England renewed his claims to the French crown in 1340 stylising himself as the 'King of England and France'. In order to hammer home the point he invaded France, successfully defeating the French navy first at the Battle of Sluys in 1340 and then her army at Crécy in 1346.

Initially the Counts of Flanders sided with the English in retribution not only for the severity of past French attacks and victories on their lands but also because it suited the Counts to guard their interests in connection with the wool trade. However after a short period it became evident that they preferred to play the English and French monarchs against one another.

During the 100 Years' War the towns of Ardres, Saint-Omer and Thérouanne were all targeted by the English (10). Saint-Omer was besieged by forces allied to Edward III in 1337 and again in 1339 under the command of the Duke of Gloucester. Both attempts failed in their attempts in taking the town.

Following the success of Edward III's defeat of the French navy at Sluys (1340) he was anxious to press home any territorial advantage on land. The Battle of Sluys fought on the 24th June completely destroyed the French fleet. This battle involved some 440 ships and the day ended with around 20 000 French dead or injured compared with only 9 000 English. The result being that La Manche or the English Channel was in English control eliminating the threat of invasion and ensuring that all future fighting could be carried out on French soil.

Edward III went on to secure the allegiance of a newly self appointed Flemish tyrant, Jan Van Artevelde (c.1290 – 1345) who was also a Burgher of Ghent with the promise that the wool trade would continue to be protected and remain an important part of Flemish business. In exchange Van Artevelde would put at Edward's disposal 150 000 Flemish troops which he could use for his summer campaign against the French. The number of soldiers proved to be a little ambitious as Van Artevalde was only able to raise a fraction of the men promised on account that he did not have the full support of all the towns in fragmented Flanders.

Undeterred Edward set about trying to raise more troops so that he would have more chance of taking Tournai. At the same time he ordered one of his close allies in the region, Robert III of Artois to take a force of 1 000 English and 11 000 Flemish troops on some light campaigning in the Artois with the aim of provoking the French into confrontation and at the very least laying siege to some of the prized fortified towns like Saint-Omer.

Meanwhile the French under the command of King Philip VI (1293 – 1350 of the Valois Dynasty) had also amassed through various recruiting schemes a considerable force of around 25 000 men. Many of whom were garrisoned in strongly fortified towns like Saint-Omer.

Robert of Artois made no secret of his intentions as his force marched purposefully in the direction of Saint-Omer. In the meantime Philip VI ordered a thousand of his knights to Saint-Omer under the command of Eudes IV, Duke of Burgundy. This force was to be backed up with more troops under the command of Jean I, Count of Armagnac.

Knowledgeable of the forthcoming hostile army, the French forces made ready for the Anglo Flemish attack. Robert and his army announced their arrival in the vicinity in true medieval style by making a lasting impression on the little town of Arques. They completely destroyed it thus giving clear indication to the citizens and garrisoned troops of Saint-Omer that he and his Flemish allies meant business. Robert of Artois hoped that his force would be welcomed by sympathizers living in Saint-Omer. This was a misguided conception.

Time however was not on Robert's side. He learnt that the considerable force under Philip VI was not too far behind his position. There was no time to lay a siege so Robert decided to present his troops in front of the walls of Saint-Omer in the hope of enticing combat. The plan worked despite the wishes of Eudes IV and Jean I who wanted to wait for Philip VI. On seeing the assembled Anglo Flemish soldiers outside the town an impatient column of French knights charged out of the gates and engaged them head on. Unbeknown to this battle hungry force they had chosen the position where the elite of Robert III's forces were situated: The ELB's (English Long Bowmen) supported by a disciplined force of soldiers from Ypres and Bergues. The French knights were quickly beaten back and on the retreat. Robert's men were obviously cock-a-hoop and fired up and so they broke ranks and followed in pursuit, leaving the relative safety of their lines and thus creating a rather dangerous 'hole' in the line. On seeing this, the French knights sniffed an opportunity so they turned on a florin and counter-attacked.

Meanwhile from the walls of Saint-Omer, the eager eyes of Eudes IV and Jean I saw the gap created by the breakaway Anglo-Flemish soldiers and they saw fit to charge out of the town with 400 of their best cavalry. Jean I forces thundered down on the already weakened flank of Robert's army. Slaughter prevailed as the French army cut through the ranks finally reaching Robert's camp where a rather disorganized and undisciplined rearguard was waiting. This too was easily routed and the resulting scene can only be summed up as a massacre.

Eudes IV on the other hand had the harder task of the two French commanders. He met with strong, disciplined and determined resistance. Fortunately unaware of the complete rout of his rearguard Robert of Artois pushed Eudes' forces back into the outlying streets to the north of Saint-Omer. A savage engagement of fighting ensued which very nearly resulted in Saint-Omer being overrun, however Eudes' forces fought bravely and finally pushed the Anglo-Flemish soldiers out of the gates. They were secured and the relieved French forces remained safely inside.

Meanwhile oblivious to the news of the near annihilation of his army at the rear Robert returned to base confronting the victorious French troops of Jean I who were making for home along the same route. Light but desperate skirmishes occurred but nothing serious enough to change the outcome of the day at any rate.

The extent of the slaughter at the rear must have been all too evident to Robert when he saw the carnage that was once his base. His forces had suffered a loss of about 8000 men that day compared to relatively few French. Realizing that he ran a very high risk of being cut down by the approaching forces of Philip VI, Robert rallied his spent force together and marched them quickly away from the area.

Militarily the battle was of little lasting importance. Territorial concerns remained the same. In the short term, confidence in the military capability of the Flemish forces was thrown into doubt. Adequate defence of southern Flanders had been weakened considerably with the high losses suffered by Robert III of Artois enabling the French to raid the Flanders countryside at will and uncontested. Finally the 'defeat' led to some Flemish towns making overtures of peace to Philip VI which had the knock on effect of denting Edward III's recruitment drive in Flanders. Despite the disappointment of the campaign Edward III remained with his initial plans and laid an unsuccessful siege against Tournai. Robert III of Artois remained a close ally of Edward and he is now buried in St Paul's Cathedral in London.

The Battle of Saint-Omer 1340 © Bibliothèque Nationale de France

The Treaty of Brétigny: 8th May 1360

The 100 Year's War rumbled on but reached a relative period of peace at the signing of the Treaty of Brétigny. This treaty was between the English and French. It secured for the English and Edward III large swathes of territory in France and also a large ransom payment of three million crowns for the safe return of the French King John II, who had been captured by Edward 'The Black Prince' at the Battle of Poitiers four years earlier in 1356. This didn't exactly happen as planned because John died in London at what was then the Hotel de Savoie but is now the site on which sits The Savoy Hotel, in 1364. In Saint-Omer there are buildings that reflect the prosperity of the town at this time amongst them being the Church of St Denis with its 13th Century tower and, in the Cathedral, the Chancel, the Ambulatory and the Transept are all from this period.

Flanders forced to embrace the House of Burgundy

Aware that the Anglo-Flemish special relationship must be maintained Edward III tried a last bit of match making to preserve it before his death in 1377 at the rather elderly age of 65. He hoped to arrange a marriage between his fifth son, John of Gaunt and the only child of Louis of Male (1330 – 1384), Marguerite III of Dampierre. However after a series of battles in which the French had driven the English from earlier territorial advantages in the north, the French King, Charles V 'The Wise' (1337 – 1380) was in a stronger position to force the hand of the ailing Louis of Male. And so in 1369 Charles The Wise arranged that Marguerite should marry non other than his brother, Philip The Bold (1342 – 1404), Duke of Burgundy thus securing the allegiance of Flanders for France. This ended the special Anglo-Flemish relationship but also saw the definitive end to rule of the region by the Counts of Flanders. And in terms of the treaty of Brétigny, after Edward III died in 1377 the French, under the command of Charles V and Philip started to dislodge the English hold over France.

Because the 100 Years' War was so far flung geographically speaking it was necessary that when military force was called for by the ruling monarchs they relied heavily on what the French term as 'Obligation Militaire' (11). This meant that all the ruling 'Bailiffs' who were answerable to the King had to supply trained and equipped soldiers for him so that he always had 'on tap' a ready fighting force. There are records that show for example that only a few days prior to the slaughter of the Battle of Agincourt in 1415 such a withdrawal on human resource took place in Saint-Omer. Here are a few of those listed from the area: Philippe de Wissocq de Saint-Omer, Robert de Guines, Philippe et Henri de Lens, Oudart de Renty and Guillaume d'Avroult. The last such demand on Saint-Omer was made in 1655 by the King of Spain.

The Black Death

Thanks largely to our furry 'Ratus Ratus' friend and fleas, Medieval Europe was plunged into the worst pandemic ever seen on planet earth – The Black Death. Between 1340 and 1351 Europe lost around 23 million people to this most horrible of afflictions. Town by town, house by house this appalling disease spread through society with no regard for wealth, education or class. The poor as always were particularly at risk of contamination and so to were doctors, priests, sailors and anyone who came into direct contact with the sick, fleas or rats. Animals were not immune either. Cattle, sheep, horses, pigs, dogs and cats to name but a few all succumbed to the rabid spread. An example of its contagiousness is shown in how it spread into Norway. This occurred as a result of a ghost ship whose crew had succumbed to the disease at sea and which was washed up on the coast near Bergen, where the rats eagerly visited (12).

The plague is recorded as entering Picardy in the summer of 1349 and spreading northward. The everyday sight of mourners and the constant presence of death severely affected the mentality and morale of everyone and to counteract this general feeling of hopelessness, desperation and despair as well as to reduce citizen contact the authorities in many towns outlawed the tolling of bells and the wearing of black and no more than two people were allowed to mourn at funerals.

Up until this time Saint-Omer had been a bustling commercial town. With the death toll rising at alarming rates the workforce was hit hard, as was the case everywhere. Cattle went untended because their keepers were dropping down dead, people were fleeing their villages and towns. For those skilled workers that remained uncontaminated the fact that they stayed alive became a real bargaining chip. It is in this vein that the textile workers of Saint-Omer around 1350 forced three pay increases in one year on account that few were left to take their place!

Like the rest of Europe Saint-Omer struggled through the plague years and changes were made within the walls of the town. The tightly packed medieval houses in their narrow streets were beginning to be dismantled and new larger residences were constructed reflecting both the status of the town and the wealth and lavish lifestyle of its traders.

Saint-Omer Rulers:	The Dukes of Burgundy
Throne of England:	Henry IV (b.1366) k.fr: 1399 – 1413
	Henry V (b.1387) k.fr: 1413 - 1422
	Henry VI (b1421) k.fr: 1422 – 1461
	Edward IV (b.1442) k.fr: 1461 – 1470
	Henry VI 1470 – 1471
	Edward IV 1471 – 1483
	Edward V (b.1470) k.fr: 1483
	Richard III (b.1452) k.fr: 1483 – 1485
	Henry VII (b.1457) k.fr: 1485 – 1509

KEY DATES

1415   Henry V trounces the French at the Battle of Agincourt

1431   St. Joan of Arc sold to the English by John of Luxembourg. Tried and martyred in Rouen by the English. Canonized in 1920.

1447   Joust organised by Duke of Burgundy for Charter of the Golden Fleece in Saint-Omer

1450's Simon Marmion paints altarpiece for l'Abbaye de St-Bertin (a part of which is in The National Gallery, London).

1453   The 100 Years War ends

1460   Tower of the Abbaye de St-Bertin is finished in a mélange of Cambresian and English architectural styles

1477   Louis XI of France besieges Saint-Omer unsuccessfully

1478   (circa) William Caxton publishes 'The Canterbury Tales' by Geoffrey Chaucer

1493   Saint-Omer is drawn into the territory of the Spanish Low Countries

The 100 Year's War continued under the reign of Henry V (1415 - 1422) who for a time was successful and as we are all aware annihilated the French army at Agincourt (*Azincourt* in French) in 1415 but the resources required to keep lands abroad proved too much and gradually the English-Plantagenet grip on their territories in France loosened and ended with their eventual expulsion from Calais in 1558. However the title of King of France for an English monarch continued right up until 1801.

There is an excellent museum telling the story of the battle at Agincourt just thirty minutes drive south from Saint-Omer.

It is important at this point in our historical journey of Saint-Omer to look at the status to which the Abbaye de Saint-Bertin had risen. It was 'The Place' to be entertained, wined and dined and for leading dignitaries to hold negotiations. In 1447 the then Duke and Duchess of Burgundy, Philip III the Good and his (3rd) wife Isabella of Portugal visited the town with the express purpose of holding a Tournament to honour those Knights who were members of the Order of the Knights of the Golden Fleece.

The Order of the Golden Fleece

Philip set up the Order of the Golden Fleece in celebration of his marriage to Isabella of Portugal (*Aviz*) in 1430 it is also a rival to the English Order of the Garter. Membership was exclusive and limited. It was open only to 'Knights' and initially there were just twenty four of them. This increased to thirty in 1433 and fifty one by 1516. Both 'Orders' were not just about shows of physical strength and skill at arms, they had an important part to play in medieval society. The key component for a successful member was Chivalry. In medieval times this meant knightly virtues, honour and courtly love.

For those of us wondering what a Knightly virtue might be (and I certainly was) here they are: courage, justice, mercy, generosity, faith, nobility and hope. Honour in this instance meant high achievement in reputation, self perception and moral identity and

46

lastly we have 'Courtly Love' which from some angles contradicts the code of moral identity!

A gathering of the Knights of the Golden Fleece © Bibliothèque de Saint-Omer

Knights belonging to the Order of the Golden Fleece or the Order of the Garter would have an obligation to the Church to become Christian Knights there to protect society and not destroy it.

The main event of Philip III's celebration of the Order of the Golden Fleece was to be a Jousting Tournament which some sources say took place near the old Calais road outside Saint-Omer. The exact location was once marked by a plaque but too many wars and historical plunderers have taken their toll to ensure that it is no longer there. Be that as it may Saint-Omer had strong membership in the Order of the Fleece. The names of the Knights associated with Saint-Omer are listed below:

Charles Duke of Orléans and Valois (1391-1465)

Jehan Duke of Brittany, Count of Montfort (1389-1442)

Jehan II Duke of Alençon, Count of Perches (1409-1476)

Jehan II King of Aragon and Navarre (1397-1479)

Adolphe le Jeune, Duke of Gueldre, Count of Zutphen (1438-1477)

Thiebault of Neufchâtel, Marshal of Burgundy (1413-1469)

Philippe Pot, Lord of La Roche de Nolay (d.1494)

Louis of Bruges, Lord of Gruuthuse (c.1422-1492)

Guy Lord of Roye (d.1463)

Mathieu of Foix, Count of Commingues (d.1453)

The banquet after the tournament was held at the Abbaye de Saint-Bertin and would have been a highly lavish and prestigious occasion. After the Tournament finished it is said by Smith-Pearse (in his Munro lecture of 1917) that the Duke wanted to do something for the locals in return so he offered them a huge Banquet and Ball - a sort of dinner dance and invited all the ladies of Saint-Omer. I wonder if this was something to do with courtly love? For some reason though none showed up and he was mightily miffed and annoyed. So, realizing their error and that they had come across as very rude the people of Saint-Omer donated £126 of medieval value money for a splendid banquet. Everybody came and the evening was apparently a great success. On show at the Musée de l'Hôtel Sandelin are three panels showing the arms of three Knights of the Order belonging to Jehan de Villiers (1430), Simon de Lalaing (1431) and Charles le Téméraire, count of Charolais (1433). These panels were originally displayed in the Abbaye de St-Bertin.

The Coat of Arms of Charles le Téméraire, Count of Charolais and Order of the Garter, knighted in 1433. The Chain of the order is clearly seen surrounding the Coat-of-Arms.
© Musée de l'hôtel Sandelin

Saint-Omer Rulers:	The Spanish

Throne of England & Wales (1536)	Henry VIII (b.1491) k.fr: 1509 – 1547
	Edward VI (b.1537) k.fr: 1547 -1553
	Lady Jane Grey (b.1537) 1553 for 9 days
	Mary 1 (b.1516) qu.fr: 1553 – 1558
	Elizabeth 1 (b.1533) qu.fr: 1558 - 1603

KEY DATES

1516   Formation of the Spanish Netherlands under Charles V of Spain

1520   Henry VIII and François I meet near Saint-Omer at the Field of the Cloth of Gold

1521   Gothic Church of Notre-Dame in Saint-Omer finally completed

1536   Anne Boleyn beheaded allegedly by a swordsman from Saint-Omer

1553   Charles V of Spain orders the destruction of the French Episcopal city of Thérouanne.

1554   Mary I labelled 'Bloody Mary' after persecution of 300 Protestants

1557   Platforms for long-range cannon constructed on walls of Saint-Omer

1558   Mary I loses Calais – last English held territory in France

1559   Saint-Omer's Egmont bastion is built

1561   Saint-Omer 'replaces' Thérouanne and is elevated to a Cathedral city

1579   Union of Utrecht

1584 – 1601 Martyrdom of 85 English and Welsh Martyrs

1584   Implication of Penal Laws and reform in England

1587   Mary Queen of Scots executed

1588   Spanish Armada routed off coast of Gravelines

1593   English Jesuits choose Saint-Omer as their centre of learning for English Catholic Men

1594   The French under the Duke of Longueville attack unsuccessfully Spanish held Saint-Omer

The majority of this century is dominated by the Spanish. Flanders was greatly influenced by events triggered by political policies and allegiances dictated by the Spanish Court. Born and bred native of Flanders, Charles V of Spain (1500 - 1558), son of Philip 1 of Spain (the Handsome) and Juana (Mad – on account of becoming mad with grief after Philip died) was not only king but also Holy Roman Emperor which gave him immense power and influence on European affairs.

Charles V was a constant rival and thorn in the side of François I (1494 – 1547) and later his son Henri II (1519 – 1559) of France and this abrasive relationship led to many conflicts and, for our interest here, led to the razing of Thérouanne in 1533. Leading up to the clashes an event was organised in which it was hoped would create an allegiance between two of the most powerful nations in Europe at the time, France and England. Today the place is referred to as The Field of the Cloth of Gold. If you come along the motorway from Calais to Saint-Omer you will see reference to this in the form of a sign '*Drap d'Or - 1520*'.

The Field of the Cloth of Gold

Henry VIII of England and François 1 met to the north of Saint-Omer (near the pretty town of Guines) in June 1520 at this Field of the Cloth of Gold. The purpose of the 'conference' was to try and become allies against Charles V of Spain and oppose his ever increasing power. Below you see the memorial that has been erected at the actual location.

At the side of the D231 is this monument commemorating the Field of the Cloth of Gold

© Photo Jonathan Caton

It is not much to write home about and, to be honest, does need a little weeding but is interesting historically. Be warned however that there is little room to park and the road can be a bit dicey so watch out for passing traffic. It is called The Field of the Cloth of Gold on account of the fact that there were tents made from huge drapes with large amounts of gold thread sewn into them.

The meeting place of wealth but not necessarily minds now commonly known as "The Field of the Cloth of Gold", depicted here by James Basire in 1774. In this field, not far from Saint-Omer, Henry VIII of England, and François I of France met in June 1520. It was François's intention to try and tempt Henry into an alliance. © 2011 Her Majesty Queen Elizabeth II

François had hoped to persuade Henry to join forces against Spain. Spain, whose stake in the Low Countries was considerable, was competing for a place to launch an attack for possession not only of England but also the New World – America. François's attempts were in vain and the outcome of the whole meeting was just a vast display of wealth, competition and merry-making. There is a popular annual event that takes place near Guines every year which re-enacts this famous meeting. For further information you should contact Ardres *Bureau de Tourisme*. Also, there is a most excellent museum in the centre of Guines called *La Tour de l'Horloge* which loosely translated means the clock tower but I think refers to a journey back in time starting with the arrival of the Vikings in Guines in the 9th Century. This relatively new museum is very hands-on and great entertainment for children of all ages (including adults) and a fabulous way to pass a couple of hours or so.

A year on after the gold dust had settled at the Cloth of Gold 'Great Exhibition', dust of the brick variety was finally settling with the long awaited completion of the church of Notre Dame in Saint-Omer. I say church because before too long events would elevate it to Cathedral status.

The Cathedral is amongst the finest in the north of France. Its magnificent 50 metre west tower in a typically English architectural style rises squarely in brilliant white limestone and crowned with four 15th Century watch-turrets is visible from almost every angle as you approach the town. The Tower houses the bells, one of which being 'Omer' peels out regularly. The sight of this Cathedral has long since greeted thousands of pilgrims and visitors over the centuries and it brought much joy to our friend Smith-Pearse when he first arrived in the town in 1917 to give his lecture on the history of the town to the Munro Institute.

He writes that the night of his arrival was dreary, cold and very damp. And his bed was too hard and small. As a result he hadn't slept too well. However on opening his shutters in the morning his spirits were instantly lifted when he saw the "glorious Cathedral and felt happier". The Cathedral has in recent years been through a massive restoration and cleaning project. Some of the external stone carvings were replaced exactly as they were hundreds of years ago. The detail is breathtaking. An example of this fabulous restoration can be seen in the photo overleaf which shows the central decoration above the door on the north side of the Cathedral.

The old with the new. A fabulously detailed piece of ornamental frieze
above the North West End Entrance. © Photo Jonathan Caton

Depending on where you are able to enter the Cathedral (it is usually accessible from at least one entrance seven days a week) will obviously dictate what you confront first. (For detailed audio guides visit the *Bureau de Tourisme* in *rue du Lion d'Or* just a five minute walk away where you can hire them). The Cathedral's basic proportions are that it is 100 metres long (the approximate length of a professional football pitch) and at its widest point is half the width of a football pitch: 30 metres. With a bit of luck you'll enter the Cathedral from the large West Door. If you do ahead of you stretches the nave, flanked by seven gothic arches and above you there is an immense organ case. The nave has three storey's consisting a series of arcades, a blind triforium and clerestory.

The nave of the Cathedral © Photo Jonathan Caton

The Cathedral nave is skirted by side chapels all featuring an array of wood and marble carvings and large oil paintings of many religious themes hanging from the walls. In the nave on the left hand side as you enter there is the tomb of Saint-Omer and almost directly adjacent from him is the 16th Century tomb of Eustache de Croy, who was Bishop of Arras and appointed Provost of Saint-Omer by Charles V of Spain. His tomb has been carved by one of the master sculptors of the day: Jacques de Broeucq of Mons.

The Astrological Clock © Photo Jonathan Caton

Among the many notable treasures of the Cathedral is a rare example of an Astrological Clock dating from 1558 by Pierre Engueran, as seen above. This is situated in the North Transept overlooking the entrance where a triumphant Louis XIV entered the Cathedral in 1677 after claiming the town for France. The clock is a masterpiece of craftsmanship and intricate engineering telling the day, date and month, the hour of the day through the twenty four hour clock and astrological information including the signs of the zodiac, the sunrise and sunset and finally the cycle of the moon. If you are present in the Cathedral on a quarter or at the half past the hour you cannot fail to hear the distinct hammer blows of '*Le Jacquemart*' or the Bell Striker who is dressed here in the traditional attire of the period except for the size of the feathers sticking out from the top of his head gear.

Le Jacquemart - Many a religious ceremony is interrupted by Le Jacquemart!

© Photo Jonathan Caton

The oldest part of the existing Cathedral is the 12th Century Chancel. Housed here is the handiwork of Charles Chifflart – one of France's leading woodcarvers of the day and also a native born in Saint-Omer, brother of the famous artist François Chifflart who was born locally in *rue de L'Arbalète* in 1825.

Examples of François Chifflart's work can be seen hanging in the former Town Hall in Place Foch, the main square, as well as a fine example of his work which resides in the Musée de l'Hôtel Sandelin – The Thieves and the Donkey painted around 1849.

Radiating Chapels with vivid and beautiful stained glass feature around the ambulatory at the East End and if one walks round from the North to the South transept you will arrive at the magnificent Lady Chapel which amongst other gems features a much venerated 13th Century Statue of Our Lady.

The Lady Chapel in the Cathedral © Photo Jonathan Caton

Other prize items in the Cathedral include a painting by Rubens of 'Christ Descending from the Cross' and also the magnificent organ.

Christ descending from the Cross by Rubens: West End of the Cathedral of Saint-Omer

© *Photo Jonathan Caton*

The organ casing by the Piette Brothers, innards by Cavaillé-Coll © Photo Jonathan Caton

Built from Danish oak this enormous 18th Century organ is lavishly decorated in the Baroque style. The casing is the work of a couple of locals – The Piette Brothers. The carvings are a wonder in themselves with the whole weighty tonnage resting, it would seem, on twelve rather spindly looking Corinthian columns and fronted by St Peter and St Paul – two of the Catholic Church's colossi. Peter holding out a large golden key to the

Church and St Paul pensively looking downwards, his golden sword unsheathed and stuck in the ground by his feet. However despite the splendour of the outside one cannot ignore the workings of this magnificent beast. The original organ was the work of Les Frères Thomas and Jean-Jacques Desfontaines who were based in Douai and finished their organ in 1717. Then in 1855 the organ received a complete overhaul from the master himself – Aristide Cavaillé-Coll (1811 – 1899). In order to give you some idea of the status of this organ builder in the organ world an apt comparison might be Mr Royce of Rolls Royce fame. Cavaillé-Coll was born in Montpellier in 1811. He is responsible for the building of some of Europe's finest organs and is recognized by many eminent composers and organists including Charles Marie Widor as being "responsible for many innovations that revolutionized the face of organ building, performance and composition" Widor himself says of him that it was "he who conceived the diverse wind pressures, the divided wind chests, the pedal systems and the combination registers ... [he] created the family of harmonic stops and perfected the mechanics to such a point that each pipe ... instantly obeys the touch of the finger .. [and is] of a quality and variety unknown before". In addition to the organ at the Cathedral of Saint-Omer completed in 1855 Cavaillé-Coll built the organs at St Denis (1841), St Sulpice, Paris (1862) – now a UNESCO World Heritage Site, Caen (1885), Toulouse (1889) and St Ouen (1890). Cavaillé-Coll was also tempted across the Channel in particular by one of the great British textile magnate's of the time John Hopwood. It was he who commissioned Cavaillé-Coll to build him an 'orgue de salon' in 1867 and then an organ for Bracewell Hall in 1870 which was later moved to Parr Hall in Warrington. Hopwood continued to champion the work of Cavaillé-Coll and he won the contract to build an organ for the Albert Hall in Sheffield in 1873. Cavaillé-Coll was also responsible for organs at the Carmolite Priory in Kensington (1866), Blackburn Parish Church (1875), St Michael's Abbey in Farnborough, Highland's College, Jersey and finally the organ at Manchester Town Hall in 1879. Other examples of his work can be found as far a field as Moscow, Mexico, Brazil and Italy. The current organ at the Cathedral of Notre Dame was classed as a historical monument in 1973 and is constantly used for both Church services and concerts. And now to return to our historical journey.

You will recall that the meeting between Henry VIII and François I has been and gone at the Field of the Cloth of Gold without any allegiance being agreed between the two countries. In fact, if anything both countries' Treasuries were the losers and additionally Henry was slightly bruised and his ego dented after he was allegedly knocked to the ground by a triumphant Francois whom he had challenged to a wrestling match.

The Destruction of Thérouanne

Meanwhile the struggle for dominance continued with Charles V over the course of the next thirteen years becoming very aggravated by the behaviour of the French in Thérouanne. Why? Firstly, it was a French town sitting in Spanish held territory, secondly, he sought 'revenge' over his disastrous Siege of Metz the year before in 1552 in which he tried and failed with a force of 80 000 men and 114 guns to retake the city from Henry II's control and finally he was so fed up with skirmishes and pillaging activities of the French forces operating out of Thérouanne that he ordered its total destruction in 1553.

Today very little remains of what was once the great Cathedral that dominated the skyline at Thérouanne. The destruction has been described by Paul Williamson in his article The Fifth Head of Thérouanne and the Problem of its original setting (13) as being carried out with "awesome efficiency". Two thousand people were employed with the specific task of dismantling the town brick by brick. The contract lasted six weeks. Destruction of the Cathedral commenced on 20th June and by the end of July hardly a trace was left. What little is left today is surrounded by a rather lovely rose garden. On the 4th July 1553 the Canons of Saint-Omer requested permission to save the Portal that you now see in the Cathedral, a figure of Christ and one of Moses. Five sculptured heads were also on the list one of which ended up as recently as 1979 in the V&A Museum in London.

The archaeological museum in the centre of Thérouanne is a little behind the times in terms of presentation and interactive technology but the welcome is warm and the contents worth seeing.

The God of Thérouanne, once 20m up on the portico of the Cathedral of Thérouanne. The figures were rescued by the Canons of Saint-Omer after Charles V of Spain ordered destruction of the Cathedral in 1553 and are now in the north transcept. © Photo Jonathan Caton

As a result of the destruction of Thérouanne the diocese of the Nord Pas-de-Calais was split three-ways: Ypres, Saint-Omer and Boulogne. The bishopric of Thérouanne passed to Saint-Omer and the church that Audomar started to build way back in 636AD was elevated to the status of Cathedral.

Amongst the transfer of ecclesiastical power and duties Saint-Omer also acquired an Irish Saint – Saint Erkembode. He now rests in the Cathedral, champion of Impossible

Causes for those suffering from physical disability, in particular children (hence the many pairs of little shoes that adorn his sarcophagus) and also those afflicted by depression.

The tomb of St Erkembode in the Cathedral of Saint-Omer. Notice the tiny pairs of shoes placed there by earnest parents © Photo Jonathan Caton

The following story is told annually in nearby Lillers in their large scale production of 'La Légende des Princes Irlandais'. It goes something like this:

Way back in the 7th Century legend has it that two young Irish Princes, Lugle and Luglien set off from Ireland destined for Rome accompanied by a number of servants. One of those servants was a man by the name of Erkembode. On their journey they would pass through many towns popular with Pilgrims. One such town was Thérouanne. Thérouanne had already a considerable reputation and it is unsurprising they wanted to pay the town a visit. However tragedy struck when they were set upon by brigands near the town. The servants fled as best they could whilst the Princes were beaten and then beheaded. Erkembode concerned for the safety and whereabouts of his masters returned to the scene where he too was set upon, beaten and left for dead. When he finally came round he witnessed the most amazing sight. Angels were taking the severed heads of his princely masters and reattaching them to their bodies. When the Bishop of Thérouanne heard Erkembode's story he was convinced of divine intervention and declared the incident a 'miracle'. The bodies of the princes were collected and to this day are honoured at three sites: Lillers, Montdidier and Ferfay. As you will no doubt have noted there are only two bodies yet three shrines. We can take it as read that as was usual with such celebrated corpses, they would have been 'dismantled' and shared out amongst numerous places of worship. Erkembode joined the religious order at Thérouanne and became its 6th Bishop (723 – 737 AD) as is recorded on the list of Thérouanne Bishops in the Cathedral.

On his death he was canonized. He was famed for his long distance ramblings as he tramped over his huge diocese. His diocese stretched from Boulogne to Ypres and to Arras.

Aside Erkembode the Cathedral and town acquired a great many other artefacts and sculptures from Thérouanne some of which can be seen in the Cathedral such as some of the ornate flagstones near the Rubens 'Christ Descending from the Cross' picture at the West End of the Cathedral.

Gérard d'Haméricourt and The Jesuits

It is during this period that a very important figure was appointed to become the second Bishop of Saint-Omer. He was Gérard d'Haméricourt. He had been the Abbot of L'Abbaye de Saint-Bertin up until his new appointment in 1562 and it was he that invited a very influential and powerful religious order to make Saint-Omer their home: The Walloon Jesuits (from Belgium) in 1567 (14). Incidentally the coats of arms of all the Bishops of Saint-Omer who were appointed by the King of France or the Pope can be seen in the north transept of the Cathedral.

Gérard d'Haméricourt as Bishop of St Bertin. He became the second bishop of Saint-Omer and invited the Walloon Jesuits to set up home in the town.

© Ms 698 Fo 6r Bibliothèque d'agglomération de Saint-Omer

The Coats of Arms for the Bishops of Saint-Omer as seen in the north transept of the Cathedral.
Gérard d'Haméricourt's Coat of Arms can be seen top row, second from the left
© *Photo Jonathan Caton*

Saint-Omer played a considerable part as a place of refuge during the religious wars and persecutions of the Reformation in England as well as the French Religious Wars of 1562 - 1598. The Jesuits (Society of Jesus) saw fit to set up their impressive college for English Catholic Men here in 1593, but more on this later. The addition of this order proved to be enormously successful and greatly added to the intellectual might of the town.

The actual town itself was chosen by the English Jesuits for a couple of reasons. Firstly, its proximity to England and secondly, there was already a considerable Jesuit community from Belgium here as we have already learned. The Jesuits were fleeing England for a key reason. This rather grim and bloody period of English history is commonly known to English Catholics as the 'Penal Times'. Between 1535 and 1681 around six hundred English, Welsh, Scottish and Irish Catholic Martyrs were put to death and some were being beatified as recently as 1987 by the then Pope, John Paul II.

Between 1584 and 1679 English Catholics were subjected to various laws forbidding and restricting Catholic practices, among them being the freedom to practise Catholicism or associate in any way with a priest or teacher of that faith. The Penal Laws were introduced periodically and as a result the periods of persecution were intermittent. The severity and execution of these laws were heavily governed by political events and military activity that became an issue of English national security.

The whole bloody episode was started by Henry VIII. He was rewarded by the Pope in Rome and made 'Defender of the Faith' after he published a book protecting the Catholic doctrine against the spread and principles of Lutherism which was at the time highly critical of the way in which mediaeval Catholicism was practised. Henry it could be said fashioned his new title from Rome as something not to dissimilar to 'Protector of his own interests' – concerning his desire for a male heir. The history of Henry and his wives is a complex and fascinating one but for our purposes we must only concern ourselves with a former mistress of the King – Anne Boleyn. She became entangled with the King as his châtelaine whilst Henry was still married to the unfortunate Catherine of Aragon. She had borne him numerous children but they either died or were girls. Henry desperately needed a male heir for reasons of succession. Unhappy that Catherine had only been able to provide him with one surviving child Mary (later Mary 1) and advancing in years he sought to marry Anne with whom he had by now fallen in love. Catherine, discovering Henry's intent to pronounce their marriage annulled (on account that he had married his dead brother Arthur's wife and thus falling foul of the teaching of Leviticus 20:21 "If a man take his brother's wife, it is an unclean thing ... they shall be childless") appealed directly to the Pope in Rome and sought council from her brother Charles V The Holy Roman Emperor at the time. In 1533 Henry's hand was forced as Anne was now pregnant. He insisted that Thomas Cranmer, Archbishop of Canterbury proclaim his marriage to Catherine as invalid. Henry married Anne Boleyn in secret in January 1533 whilst Catherine kept her life but not her crown. She was pushed aside and died shortly afterwards in 1536. Ironically 1536 was not a good year for either Catherine or Anne. We know after Anne fell out of favour with Henry and was sentenced to death, the swordsman appointed by royal nod to carry out the execution was, according to some sources from Saint-Omer, others cite Calais. As a matter of note it is interesting that Anne was given the option of beheading by the sword in contrast to the clumsier English axe because she was a Queen and therefore held that right. Had she been any old traitor (as she was charged to be, in addition to incest and adultery) she would have been burnt. We know that she showed great courage leading up to the moment of her death from the account left to us by Sir William Kingston, Constable of the Tower of London. He writes of the grim event:

"This morning she sent for me, that I might be near her at such time as she received the good Lord, to the intent I should her speak as touching her innocency always to be dear. And in the writing of this she sent for me, and at my coming she said: "Mr Kingston, I hear I shall not die afore noon, and I am very sorry therefore, for I thought to be dead by this time and past my pain." I told her it should be no pain, it was so little.[Her neck that is] And then she said: "I heard say the executioner was very good, and I have a little neck," and then put her hands about it, laughing heartily.

She wore a red petticoat under a loose dark grey gown of damask trimmed with fur. Her dark hair was bound up and she wore on this occasion an English style gable hood and her customary French headdress. She made a short speech:

"Good Christian People. I am come hither to die, for according to the law, and by the law I am judged to die, and therefore I will speak nothing against it; I am come hither to accuse no man, nor to speak anything that, where of I am accused and condemned to die, but I pray God Save the King and send him long to reign over you, for a gentler nor a more merciful prince was there never: and to me he was ever a good, a gentle and sovereign Lord. And if any person will meddle of my cause, I require them to judge the best. And thus I take my leave of the world and of you all, and I heartily desire you all to pray for me. O Lord have mercy on me, to God I commend my soul."

The swordsman, and there is no known record of his name, was paid £23 6s.8d for his services. When I observed the enormity of the sum in those times to one of the research librarians at the 'Bibliothèque de Saint-Omer' she looked at me slightly affronted and exclaimed "Well! She was a Queen!". Point taken. In comparison to modern day values this would equate to about £8,000.

In any case with Papal permission from Rome for an annulment refused, Henry set himself up as "the supreme head of the Church in England" and married again. Two of the most notable first martyrs are Sts Thomas More – Henry's Lord Chancellor and John Fisher, Cardinal and Archbishop. Both of whom strongly objected to Henry's self-appointment as Head of the Church in England. When Henry died he was succeeded by his son Edward VI and there was little suppression of the Catholics. In 1553 Edward VI died and was succeeded by Mary 1. Now she was a Catholic and had every intention of restoring Roman Catholicism as England's national faith before Henry had decided otherwise. She succeeded in part (though the Church of England was popular by now and Anglicans were not keen to return to the Holy Church of Rome under the authority of the Pope) but Mary only lived for another five years. Yet in her short reign she married, unsurprisingly, Phillip II of Spain who was a Catholic. A marriage that proved highly unpopular in England and also earned herself the name 'Bloody Mary' by her association with the killing of 300 Protestants. She died in 1558 and was succeeded by Anne Boleyn's only child; Elizabeth who reigned from 1558 – 1605.

Elizabeth I was a strict Protestant and she quickly swung the national faith back to Canterbury and the Church of England and there it has stayed ever since. During the early years of her reign suppression of Catholics was not too evident but events were about to change all that.

An unsuccessful revolt by Catholics in the North of England in 1569 protesting against The Church of England and what they saw as the illegal imprisonment of Mary Queen of Scots, who in their eyes was the rightful heir to the throne and not Elizabeth, sparked off fears that religious instability and all its unpleasantness was bubbling under the surface. This event was followed by Elizabeth's excommunication by Pope St Pius V in 1570 who decreed that all her subjects 'be released from their allegiance to her' – a highly provocative decree.

In England two acts of Parliament were passed in 1593 further prohibiting the movements of Catholics who were found guilty of recusancy, which was a refusal to worship in accordance with the customs of the Church of England. The penalty for this was confiscation for life of all property, possessions and land. The second act was against those who helped seminary priests such as Jesuits who started to arrive in England during the 1570's. The penalty for those caught mixing with, giving shelter to or aiding these men was the charge of treason. The punishment at this time for treason was quite simple – being killed in a most gruesome, excruciatingly painful and hideous manner. Normally this meant being hung, drawn and quartered with lots of people milling about enjoying the spectacle.

Suspicions of pacts between Catholics, Spaniards and Rome reached boiling point in 1588 when the Spanish Armada was routed off the coast of Gravelines near Dunkerque.

It was a considerable force that had been assembled on the orders of King Phillip II of Spain. The invasion force comprised 130 ships, 20 000 soldiers and 8 500 sailors. For 16 years after this most celebrated victory and the removal of the threat of invasion Catholic persecution was intense. As a result between 1584 and 1601 eighty-five martyrs were put to death for their faith – many having passed through the Jesuit College for English men in Saint-Omer.

The Stonyhurst College Quadruple Crest showing the double cross used in the town's own Coat-of-arms at its head © Stonyhurst College

One other proposed Act that in fact never became law was "that the children of Catholic parents should be removed after the age of seven from their parents' care and placed, at their parents' expense, in the homes of approved Protestants, to be brought up in the Queen's religion" (15). Added to the persecutions *'déjà fait'*, news of this intended

74

Act reached the ears of the Jesuits in Spain a certain Father Robert Persons who was already renowned for his work in Rome, England and Spain and who set himself the task of creating a school whereby English Catholic boys could be educated. Persons had already been involved in setting up an English School within an existing school at Eu in Normandy but this was neither orthodox in Jesuit teaching nor headed by a Jesuit. So without fuss the Jesuits settled in Saint-Omer (the school's name known as St Omers to those in England) initially sharing premises and classes with the Belgium Jesuits of the Walloon College.

Father Persons – founder of the English Jesuit College of St Omers © Stonyhurst College

The first intake of fifteen boys was rather small but that was all that the accommodation would allow. The school had to be self-financing so an annual bursary or 'pension' was secured from the Spanish court. However this turned out to be a haphazard obligation and finance was a constant headache for the head of the school or Rector as he is known in Jesuit circles. Over the 169 years that the English Jesuit College remained in Saint-Omer it grew in size and reputation at an impressive speed. Indeed, after only a few years following their arrival the pupil numbers grew sufficiently that they were able to acquire an impressively large plot situated on rue Saint-Bertin where the old Hotel de Regnauville had once stood. The hotel and land were purchased (amid some local opposition) thanks to the skilful negotiations of the second Rector: Father Giles Schondonch. By all accounts a highly capable human being and a huge inspiration to the development of the College. Schondonch was the longest serving Rector at St Omers with a watch lasting sixteen years and is considered as one of the leading forces for the advancement and preservation of the educational tradition of St Omers along with two other notables: Fr Roger Lee, Master and Confessor of St Omers for eight years and the appropriately named Fr Thunder (some sources cite Tunder which doesn't have quite the same effect) who was 'Prefect of the Boys' and "Praefectus Studiosorum" or Head of Studies and a man described as "of grave and mature mould [with] a genial disposition" (16). As a result of a severe fire in 1684 which pretty much destroyed the old school buildings that Fr Schondonch had been responsible for, they built one of the most impressive buildings in the town which can be seen today in Rue Saint-Bertin.

The former English Jesuit College of St Omers as seen today in rue St-Bertin

© Photo Jonathan Caton

The chapel of the Walloon Jesuits although badly in need of restoration nowadays is still worthy of a visit. Visible from miles around towering over the town it is situated in rue du Lycée but more on this later.

The Chapel of the Walloon Jesuits in Saint-Omer located in rue du Lycée

© *Photo Jonathan Caton*

It is worth noting at this point the high demands placed on the young students. A typical day at St Omers would be something like this:

5.00	Rise and shine - on Sundays and Feast Days a 'lie-in' was permitted until 5.30am. This was referred to as a 'Long Sleep'.
5.00 – 5.15	Washing, dressing and making of bed
5.15 – 5.30	Private meditation

5.30 – 6.00	Mass
6.00 – 7.00	Morning Studies
7.00 – 7.15	Breakfast – Continental style
7.15 – 7.30	Recitation in classrooms
7.30 – 10.00	Lessons with a Master
10.00 – 10.15	'Necessites naturae' and discussion allowed in Greek or Latin
10.15 – 11.00	Private Study
11.00 – 11.30	Dinner
11.30 – 12.30	Recreation. In summer half an hour would be dedicated to music
12.30 – 12.45	Short break
12.45 – 13.45	Private Study
13.45 – 16.30	Lessons
16.30 – 16.45	'Bread and Beer' – a ritual that continued at Stonyhurst until 1908
16.45 – 18.30	Night Studies
18.30 – 19.00	Supper
19.00 – 20.00	Recreation. In winter the music séance was straight after supper
20.00 – 20.30	Private Study
20.30 – 20.45	Night prayers - kneeling at their desks
20.45 – 21.00	Notices and thoughts for meditation
21.00	Snuff out candles and bed, thank goodness!

I am pleased to add that this very strenuous regime was regularly interspersed with half day holidays and during the summer (after 1626) the students were able to enjoy the delights of 'Villa House'. This was a small country house in nearby Blendecques (3km south from Saint-Omer) or as they would have known it Blandyke or Whyte Banks. To this day exeats are still referred to at Stonyhurst as Blandyke days.

Pupils from both the Walloon College and St Omers progressed through the school with class names closely linked to subjects classified as 'Humanities'. The entry level class was known as Figures which went onto 'Grammar' then 'Syntax' followed by 'Poetry' and finally arriving at 'Rhetoric' – that most skilful form of human communication. Shared classes between the two colleges ceased in 1614. Music and drama formed an important part of the curriculum and regular performances were put on that were noted far beyond the reach of the town. We know that St Omers was a popular destination for visitors and travellers passing through the area and the College enjoyed entertaining a veritable stream of guests, "clerical and lay, statesmen, scholars, soldiers and others, both Catholic and non-Catholic" sadly none of this helped to off-set the amount of debt that the college incurred but it did add further notoriety to the colleges and town. In terms of pupil numbers St Omers reached its peak in 1635 when there were two hundred pupils studying at the school.

Along with the other religious denominations in the town they were highly versatile and an asset. In times of conflict, famine and disease the local community relied upon the guidance, charity and help of all the religious establishments. One such period was between 1635 and 1638 when the town of Saint-Omer went through bouts of recurring pestilence - some sources claim that eight thousand people died as a result of infection during this time. One notable casualty being afore mentioned Fr Thunder who died in September 1638 as a result of a plague. It was also a period when military activity in the area was prevalent between the French and Spanish. Saint-Omer was besieged for a six week period in 1638 by Gaspard de Coligny and a force of twenty-five thousand French troops. This resulted in an influx of people into the town – all of whom needed food and shelter particularly from those fleeing the small towns and villages dotted around Saint-Omer like Watten and Blandyke for as usual they were sacked with gusto. Then as a result of the fall of Hesdin (pronounced Ay Dan (as in the name Dan except with a silent 'n') to the French a year later, or 1639, the number of inhabitants increased again because of the refugees from there and around taking refuge in Saint-Omer thus testing the already dwindling resources of the town and its religious communities. St Omers for example fed an additional hundred plus people three times a week during this period and if you think about it that's a lot of additional soup and bread when you can't just pop out to Sainsbury's, or in the case of this area Auchan or Carrefour, for provisions. During periods of conflict (which as we know there were many) sources tell us that on several occasions the pupils of St Omers and the Walloon College helped mend or build defensive walls.

Before we depart St Omers College or more fitting would be to say before St Omers quit the town as a result of the 'arrêt' from Paris in 1762, it is appropriate that I briefly bring to your attention the small town of Watten (pronounced Wat). Watten lies about five miles north of Saint-Omer and here was a Preparatory School that at one time belonged to the Jesuits. Situated on top of the hill one can still see the once proud and lofty Abbey tower that dominated the Watten skyline.

What remains was originally built in the 11th Century by the crusading Count of Flanders Robert II for the Canons Regular of St Augustine. The Abbey was dedicated to Our Lady on account of the fact that they had in their procession a rare and most precious relic – a lock of hair from The Virgin Mary which had been given to them in 1097 by Clemence the Countess of Flanders, wife to Robert II – who had brought it back from Jerusalem. The Abbey's history and transition into the hands of the Jesuits is a complex one so I will not go into great depth on the subject; suffice to say that I will try to be brief, accurate and clear. As we have already learned it was customary for marauding armies to sack and pillage towns and villages wherever they went. Watten was no exception and by the time the Abbey had again been sacked, this time by the French in 1577 the remaining inhabitants were only seven 'old, decrepit and unedifying' Canons who fled to the safety of Saint-Omer and a 'safe-house' that they knew of in rue St Bertin. The Abbey had been in decline for some time and the Bishop of the day – Bishop Blaise (his stint being 1600 – 1618) had run out of options as to the future of the crumbling heap as far as he could see. No-one wanted it despite offers of ownership made to the Dominicans and indeed to Blaise's own order, the Franciscans. So what to do? A situation now conveniently presented itself in the form of the English Jesuits. Before Saint-Omer had been selected by Fr Persons as home to the College, the Spanish city of Bilbao had been bandied about as a suitable place to set up the college. This was not a popular choice with Fr Persons who argued that Bilbao however beautiful and convenient for the Spanish Court, was however too far from England and in his view the climate was inappropriate for the English temperament. Not a man to let matters rest Fr Persons wrote to Fr Schondonch from Rome asking him to seek out a more suitable place in the North. The subject was aired on one of Fr Schondonch's regular visits (17) to Bishop Blaise who then experienced a 'eureka' moment and offered the property to the Society of Jesus who readily accepted. The negotiations for the takeover became very complex involving a Pope, a King, an Archduke, a Bishop, an Ambassador and Fr Schondonch and it was not until 8 August 1611 some eight years later that Fr Schondonch finally got hold of the keys. The Abbey initially became the home for the Belgian Jesuits but in 1623 thirty English novices took residence and stayed there until their departure in 1765 save for a few occasions when the residents had to flee for their lives back to the safety of St Omers which is where we will briefly return.

Following is a list of some of the former rectors and pupils that have been assembled by Mr H Piers in his book "Anecdotes Anglaises sur la ville de Saint-Omer' printed in 1847 as well as some others. As we already know many of these students form part of English and Welsh Martyrs. The following from the list were Rectors:

Fr William Baldwin (1563 – 1632) specialist on meditation and Rector of St Omers 1621 – 1632

Fr Charles Plowden was a prolific writer and he entered the Society of Jesus in 1759, and was ordained priest, at Rome, in 1770. From 1774 onwards Father Plowden had much to do with the establishment of Stonyhurst College in Lancashire and indeed became its first Rector in 1817.

Father Charles Plowden and overleaf Stonyhurst College in Lancashire. © Stonyhurst College

Fr Thomas Stapleton (b. Henfield in Sussex and in Leuven, Belgium d.1598) Controversial theologian and writer. He took a prominent role in the creation of the English College at Douai. He was appointed Rector of St Omers between 1679 – 1683. His many literary works were reprinted as four tomes in Paris in 1620.

The following are some of the Pupils from St Omers:

Blessed Arthur Bell, also known as Francis Bell. He entered St Omers College around 1614 later to join the Franciscans. He was hung, drawn and quartered in London on 11 December 1643 for his faith. He was beatified by Pope John Paul II in 1987

Alban Butler born c.1709 at Appletree in Northamptonshire. Author of the acclaimed 'Lives of the Fathers, Martyrs and other principal Saints'. He was ordained as a priest in 1735.

Daniel Carroll (1730 – 1796) Maryland Delegate and one of the Founding Fathers of the United States. He studied at St-Omers between 1742 and 1748 following in his older brother's footsteps, John Carroll.

John Carroll born in 1735 he joined the Jesuits in St Omers in 1735. He was ordained a priest in 1769. After the suppression of the Jesuit college at Liege he went to Maryland in the USA and ended up becoming the America's first Catholic Bishop and Archbishop. He died in 1815.

Charles Carroll was born in 1737 and was part of a veritable dynasty of Carrolls who received their education at St Omers – ten in total. Like his ancestors Charles Carroll made his fortune in America becoming one of its richest citizens. This wealth proved instrumental in helping to keep afloat the aspirations of those fighting under George Washington against George III of England in the War of Independence. Firmly and accountable on the winning side Charles Carroll was the only Catholic signatory of the Declaration of Independence on 4 July 1776. A statue of him can be found in the Hall of Columns in the United States Capitol. Despite living to the mighty age of 95 he was active enough five years before his death to advise on the creation of one of America's first railroads – Baltimore to Ohio and lay its cornerstone at the opening Ceremony on March 8th 1827.

Charles Carroll of Carrollton by Sir Joshua Reynolds, c.1763 oil on canvas

© Yale Center for British Art, Paul Mellon Collection B1981.25.521

Herbert Croft born c.1603 in Hereford. Once chaplain to King Charles I and author of 'Le Vertitable état de la primitive Eglise'.

Saint Philip Evans born in Monmouth in 1645. He joined the Jesuits in 1665 at Watten. He returned to his native Wales as a Missionary in 1675 but became fatally embroiled with a fellow priest St John Lloyde in what is known as the Popish Plot instigated by the "extremely odious and equally dangerous" Titus Oates – that "lecherous and dedicated liar" – a former pupil of St Omers (albeit for a few months) he went on to busy himself in fabricating evidence and causing the ultimate and untimely deaths of so many of his peers. Two of them being St Philip Evans and St John Lloyde who were executed together at Cardiff on 5th May 1679. Close to the moment of execution Philip Evans is reputed to have turned to Father Lloyde and said "Adieu Father Lloyde! Though only for a short time, for we shall soon meet again." To which Father Lloyde replied "I never was a good speaker in my life." The pair were canonized in 1970 by Pope Paul VI.

Saint Thomas Garnet, the first martyr also known as protomartyr of St Omers executed at Tyburn at the age of 32 in 1608. He was one of the first students at the College. His relics were in Saint-Omer but were lost in the French Revolution of 1789. He was canonized in 1970 by Pope Paul VI.

Stained glass from Stonyhurst of Sts Thomas Garnet and Philip Evans

Charles Alban Gibbes, son of a Bristolian doctor, author of a book on Medicine in 3 volumes. Died in Rome in 1677.

Charles Gildon b.1666 was a translator, biographer, essayist, playwright, poet, author of fictional letters, fabulist, short story writer and critic. He became Editor of *The British Mercury* - a newspaper of the time. He died on 1st January 1724.

Charles Gooden Maths Teacher.

William Habington (1605 – 1654) English poet who published amongst others three volumes of Poetry (1634 – Castara, Vol 2 in 1635 and Vol 3 in 1640) and a series of essays at the time called 'Observations on History' printed in 1641.

Blessed William Ireland was admitted to the Society of Jesus at Watten in 1655; professed, 1673; and was for several years confessor to the Poor Clares at Gravelines. He was executed during the reign of King Charles II for participating in the alleged but fabricated "Popish plot" against the king. He was beatified in 1929.

Saint John Lloyde originally from Brecon. He was a Philosophy and Theology teacher and author of The Life of Brunehaut – a study in which he tries to justify the crimes of this Visigoth princess! The book is called 'Vita Brunichildis Francorum Reginae' and was at the time of Pier's publication available to view in the Bibliothèque de Saint-Omer. He was executed with St Phillip Evans in Cardiff on 5th May 1679.

Arthur Murphy (1730 – 1805) Barrister, journalist, actor, biographer, translator and playwright. Described as a dramatic Irish poet of the 18th Century who also wrote under the pseudonym 'Charles Ranger'. He is thought to have coined the legal term 'wilful misconstruction'. He was placed in the College of St Omers by his aunt who lived in Boulogne.

Portrait of Arthur Murphy by Nathanial Dance painted in 1777

© National Portrait Gallery, London

Leonard Neale was born in 1746 in Maryland USA. He was the fifth child of thirteen children to William Neale and his wife Anna. At the age of 12 he was sent to St-Omers to study. Completing his studies he entered the Society in Ghent in 1767. His pastoral vocation took him to England, British Guiana and finally back to America where he was made Bishop in 1800. Here he worked fervently with Bishop Carroll and one of his brothers Fr Charles Neale SJ to strengthen the Society in the States. He died on June 18 1817 in Georgetown and was described by Bishop Carroll as "a man truly pious, endowed with the highest prudence, humility and suavity of manner and highly skilled in ecclesiastical learning and discipline." He is reputed, as there is no concrete evidence, to have baptized George Washington on his deathbed in 1799.

Thomas Phillips was born around 1708. Author of a fascinating subject concerning The History of the life of Reginald Pole (printed in 2 Volumes by William Jackson Oxford 1764). Pole was an English Cardinal during the times of Henry VIII and was the last Catholic archbishop of Canterbury.

Saint John Plessington Educated at St-Omers and Valladoid. Ordained in Sergovia in 1662. He was arrested on his return to England and caught up in the scare of the Popish Plot. He was hung, drawn and quartered at Boughton, near Chester in July 1679. He was canonized in 1970 by Pope Paul VI.

Francis Plowden (1749 – 1819). Barrister and writer. He was awarded the title of Doctor of Civil Law by the University of Oxford which was some considerable achievement as he was a known practicing Catholic. Some of his literary works include: An Historical Review of the State of Ireland, from the Invasion of that Country by Henry II, to Its Union with Great Britain on the First of January 1801 (London: C. Rowarth 1803); The History of Ireland, from the Invasion under Henry II to its Union with Great Britain (1809); The History of Ireland, from its Union with Great Britain, in January 1801, to October 1810 (1811). On route from Rome in 1821 where he had been involved in the election of 'The Superior General for the Society' he died suddenly. He was given a full military burial because the local authorities assumed he was an army General in their miscomprehension of the type of 'General' he had been in discussion about in Rome. His funeral took place at Jougne on the Swiss Border in France!

Joseph Simons was born in Hampton c.1594 Specialised in the Humanities and Philosophy.

Fr Henry Thunder was born in Kent c.1572 d 1638. A former pupil of St Omers he returned in 1615 to take up his post as Prefect of Discipline. He is regarded as being one of the leading lights of St Omers College and valued as a priest with "admirable piety and candour".

William Wright was born in York 1562 d London 1639. Although listed in Piers as having studied at St-Omers some sources cite that he received some of his education at the English College in Rome. Following his education he became Professor of Philosophy at Gratz and Vienna Universities. On his return to England he was appointed as the Chaplain for the Gage family at Hengrave Hall in Suffolk. Following the Gunpowder Plot of 1605, and also because his employers were known recusants, he was arrested and spent time in both the Tower of London and White Lion Prison. He tended to the sick and dying in this establishment during the plague. Many of his literary works came after 1612. In addition he wrote translations of the works of Becan and Lessius.

Below is a list of the Rectors of the English Jesuit College of St Omers between 1593 and 1762 when the college left for Bruges. The dates indicate the year in which they started their 'Rectorship'.

William Flack (Superior) (1593), Jean Foucart (1594), Giles Schondonch (1600), Philippe Dennetiers (1617), William Baldwin (1621), Thomas Worsley (1632), Thomas Port (1636), Edward Courtney (1646), Henry More (1649), Charles d'Arcy (1652), Thomas Babthorpe (1656), Henry More bis (1657), Richard Barton (1660), Thomas Carey (1669), Richard Ashby (1678), Thomas Stapleton (1678), John Warner (1683), Michael Constable (1688), Edward Petre (1693), William Walton (1697), Henry Humberston (1701), Edward Slaughter (1705), Richard Plowden (1709), Louis Sabran (1712), Francis Powell (1715), William Darell (1720), John Turberville (1721), James Gooden (1722), Richard Plowden (1725), Richard Hyde (1728), Thomas Eccleston (1731), Joseph Constable (1737), Percy Plowden (1739), Richard Hyde (1742), Charles Wells (1745), Nathaniel Elliott (1748), John Darell (1752), Francis Scarisbrick (1759).

St Omers College remained as an educational establishment at its site in rue St Bertin even after the Jesuits departed in 1762. It served as a Hôpital Militaire opening its doors for those wounded at the Battle of Hondschoote in 1793. It remained in this medical role right up to the end of World War Two in 1945. The building and surrounding premises have now returned to education and form part of the reputable Lycée Alexandre Ribot (after Alexandre Ribot 1842 – 1923, a native of Saint-Omer who became French Prime Minister no less than four times).

If you are interested in learning in far greater depth the fascinating history of the Jesuits in Saint-Omer and their transition through Bruges, Liege and finally Stonyhurst I thoroughly recommend that you read "St Omers to Stonyhurst" by Hubert Chadwick SJ and look out for a forthcoming book by Professor Maurice Whitehead (School of Arts and Humanities: History and Classics at Swansea University) who has carried out extensive research on the Carroll family and the Jesuits.

The Walloon Jesuits

The Walloon Jesuits arrived in Saint-Omer in 1567. They came from Wallonia which is in effect southern Belgium. The Chapelle de Jesuits is one of the most impressive buildings of Saint-Omer but sadly one of the most neglected. Since the Jesuits left Saint-Omer in 1762 the Chapel had very mixed fortunes in terms of use and it is rather miraculous that it has survived at all. It still is a marvellous space and I encourage you to visit it. There are often notable art exhibitions held there. Below is a potted history of the Chapel's rise and fall over the centuries.

1567	Walloon Jesuits set up home in Saint-Omer at the invitation of Gérard d'Haméricourt, Bishop of Saint-Omer.
1615	Using the design of Mons architect Jean de Blocq building of the new chapel begins.
1629	The main Chapel is completed built from red brick and stone.
1640	The two towers are finished completing the Chapel.
1762	Walloon and English Jesuits kicked out of Saint-Omer.
1762	In effect the chapel was deconsecrated and became a *Magasin de Fourrage* or storage for fodder.
1811	Reverted back to the Church.
1870 – 1871	Turned into a barracks for the army.
1914 – 1918	Served as a Military Hospital.
1942	Declared a historic monument.
1945	The chapel became a garage and a salle de sport – parking divisions in paint still visible.
2013	Massive restoration project on the exterior.

Today the Chapel comes under the jurisdiction of the *'Animation du Patrimoine'* and plays host to many art exhibitions and occasional concerts.

Notable alumni of the Walloon Jesuit College include Pierre Alexandre de Monsigny (1729 - 1817). He was a French composer, and considered founder of the new musical genre of his day, the 'Opéra Comique'. A leading French 19th century composer is quoted as saying of him: "Of all the composers of our country, he may be the first who had the gift of true, human emotion, of communicative expression and of fair feeling."

French composer Pierre Alexandre de Monsigny - former pupil of the Walloon Jesuit College, Saint-Omer. This statue by the noted sculptor Louis Noël can be found just below the Cathedral of Saint-Omer in Place Sithieu. © Photo Jonathan Caton

The Jesuit Chapel © Jonathan Caton

| Saint-Omer Rulers: | The Spanish up to 1678 |
| | The French 1678 onwards |

Throne of England:	James 1 (b.1566) 1603 – 1625
& Wales	Charles 1 (b.1600) 1625 – 1649
	Oliver Cromwell - Lord Protector (b.1599) 1653 – 1658
	Richard Cromwell - Lord Protector 1658 - 1659
	Charles II (b.1630) 1660 - 1685
	James II (b.1633) 1685 – 1688
	William III 'of Orange' (b.1650) 1689 – 1702

KEY DATES

1611   Saint-Omer strengthens its defences by constructing bastions and demi-lunes.

1611   Cromwell and an Expeditionary Force join the French and lay waste the countryside around Saint-Omer.

1615   Walloon Jesuits start building Chapel in Saint-Omer.

1616   William Shakespeare dies on 23rd April.

1630   Tobacco is first grown in Clairmarais.

1635   English Jesuit College: St Omers at peak with 200 pupils.

1638   French Army under Gaspard de Coligny besiege Saint-Omer – attempt fails.

1638   Plague kills 8000 in Saint-Omer.

1639   Hesdin (50 kms south of Saint-Omer) falls to the French.

1659   French expand into Spanish held lowlands through the terms reached in the Treaty of the Pyrénées.

1660   First tobacco grower sets up in Saint-Omer.

1666   The Saint-Michel fort built at Saint-Omer.

1666   Saint-Omer besieged by the French under command of Marshal de Chastillon – attempt failed.

1677   Saint-Omer is taken by Louis XIV's brother - Philippe Duc of Orléans .

1678   The Peace of Nijmegen and Saint-Omer becomes French.

1679   Penal Time ends in England.

As we can see from our events in history above the 17th Century was a period of great development for Saint-Omer. The first seventy-eight years Saint-Omer continued to be ruled by the Spanish but from 1678 this changed to France. On the industrial front a major and wealth accruing enterprise was about to settle on Saint-Omer and its environs – tobacco.

Tobacco which was known throughout Europe since Christopher Columbus introduced it in 1492 where it gradually gained a reputation for being the miracle and universal cure for many illnesses and disorders. From 1630 Tobacco was introduced into the cultivated fields of Clairmarais with great success. However it is not until the 18th Century that Pipe production in Saint-Omer made a European name for itself. So with this in mind we will delve further into Saint-Omer and its strong associations with smoking a little further up the time line.

Aside the commercial and religious aspects of the wealth of Saint-Omer the town also had unlimited and abundant access to two commodities that fuelled the production of early printing: water and cloth - both basic components of early forms of paper production. It is little wonder that Saint-Omer and its surrounding area had many paper mills and to this day some of the largest providers of employment in the surrounding area are connected with paper and packaging manufacture. For example at nearby Wizernes is the factory of Arjo Wiggins another historic firm is Avot-Vallée in Blendecques who have one of the oldest working mills in the area – over one hundred and thirty years old. It is worth bringing to your attention at this point the excellent museum called *Maison du Papier* just outside Wizernes which traces the history of Paper production and gives visitors the chance of making their own. However, in returning to our historical journey, it is a point of interest that up until 1600 very little had actually been printed. We know by the vast collection of the beautifully illuminated manuscripts which are now available to view by appointment in the *Salle du Patrimoine* at the *Saint-Omer Bibliothèque* that the monks and scribes had been very busy in the various '*Abbayes*' but in terms of grasping the concept of mass production, progress was surprisingly slow considering the first printing presses were operating in Germany around 1440 thanks to the likes of Johannes Gutenberg.

It was only in 1602 that a certain Francis Bellet set up shop in what was then *rue Tenne Rue*. This street is now the busiest commercial street in the town; rue de Dunkerque. He left seven years later taking the latest printing technology with him to Ypres. However that was not the end because his departure almost coincided with the English Jesuits cranking up their own clandestine Press and as might be expected they wasted no time in printing a huge number of volumes tackling an array of subjects from banned Catholic texts, works warning of the dangers of Protestantism, historically themed subjects and a variety of other texts as we have already seen in the section covering St Omers College. Around the middle of the seventeenth century the religious communities printing presses were joined in harmony by the commercial printing business of Simon Ogier whose rather splendid house can be found at *99 rue de Dunkerque* – a house that he acquired in 1685. It is worth noting that in the *Bibliothèque de Saint-Omer* there are magnificent and rare pages from the Gutenberg bible dating from around 1450 as well as a rare example of the original complete encyclopaedia of D'Alembert and Diderot printed around 1750.

During this turbulent period the defences of the town were further enhanced with the addition of demi-lune shaped projections as well as the Saint-Michel Fort built in 1666. Yet despite these additional defences Saint-Omer finally succumbed to the armies of Louis XIV and the king's brother, Philippe Duc d'Orléans in April 1677.

A year later much of the Spanish Low Countries and the Franche-Comté transferred to Louis XIV '*Le Roi Soleil*' or Sun King at the Treaty of Nijmegen signed on

17th September 1678. The victorious Louis XIV and his entourage visited the town in 1677 and again in 1680 this time accompanied by his wife. He entered the Cathedral via the North Transept door which back then would have had direct access to the Bishop's residence which is now the *Palais de Justice*. There is a picture by Hippolyte Joseph Cuvelier which hangs in the *Hôtel de Ville* (*Place Foch*) which depicts Louis XIV in the Cathedral of Saint-Omer at around this time.

With the change in ownership came a change in architectural style. Out with the Flemish and Spanish (there are many examples of Spanish buildings in the town one being the *La Barre Barracks* on the *Esplanade*) and in with the French of the day. With the continued growing prosperity of the town there was a need to rebuild and replace buildings in the glorious style of architecture that emanated from the streets of Paris. And that is what you see in many of the buildings still in existence today. There is no better example of this new classical style than the *Musée de l'hôtel Sandelin*, once the private winter residence of the Countess of Fruges. Tragically for her it was only a home for ten years, the ownership being somewhat terminated by the French Revolution. The Countess kept her head and fled to Spain, but we will learn more about the actual building of *l'hôtel Sandelin* later on.

Saint-Omer Rulers:	France – First Republic 1792 - 1804
Throne of England:	Anne (b.1665) 1702 – 1714
Wales & Scotland (1707)	George 1 (b.1660) 1714 – 1727
	George II (b.1683) 1727 – 1760
	George III (b.1738) 1760 – 1820

KEY DATES

1702 – 1713	Spanish Wars of Succession – 40 000 dead.
1708	Marlborough besieges and captures Lille.
1709	Mass famine in France.
1710	Marlborough besieges and takes Aire-sur-la-lys.
1713	Treaty of Utrecht signed.
1726	English Jesuit School in rue St-Bertin under construction.
1727	Isaac Newton dies on 31st March.
1750	Seventeen tobacco producers in Clairmarais.
1751	Saint-Omer porcelain production begins.
1762	English Jesuits leave St Omers College.
1775	Construction begins on l'hôtel Sandelin for the Countess of Fruges.
1783	Horatio Nelson stays in Saint-Omer.
1783	America wins War of Independence.
1789	The French Revolution – Saint-Omer loses its ecclesiastical clout.
1789	Tobacco production at its peak with 28 manufacturers in Clairmarais.

European peace and stability were very volatile during the 17th and 18th centuries. A power struggle had developed between Spain and France which influenced greatly other European powers namely England, the Holy Roman Empire and the United Provinces of the Netherlands. One of the major conflicts during this time was the War of Spanish Succession which lasted from 1702 – 1713 at a cost of about forty thousand lives. The objective of this war was to stop France and Spain forming an alliance due to the 'will' of Charles II of Spain, who wished that all his possessions, including his kingdom, pass to Philip Duc d'Anjou. He was later to become Philip V of Spain. How could Philip claim the French territories as well? He happened to be the grandson of Louis XIV of France and in line to inherit or at least lay claim to France. Who was against this succession? Pretty much everyone outside the aforementioned kingdoms. This said the Spanish were thrown into doubt over the legitimacy of the inheritance and instead had a Civil War.

Leopold I of Hapsburg who was Holy Roman Emperor was very against this especially as he laid claim to the Spanish territories himself. After what is alleged to have been a slow start to the conflict, Hapsburg was joined by England, Portugal and the Dutch Republic which basically constituted most of Belgium, Luxembourg and the Low Countries.

The fighting took place over a vast geographical area: Spain, Germany, Italy, Colonial North America (also known as Queen Anne's War) and in the Low Countries. It was here in the Nord Pas-de-Calais and Low Countries that two generals distinguished themselves as master tacticians: The Duke of Marlborough and Prince Eugène of Austria. The war was concluded in 1713 with the Treaty of Utrecht and the Treaty of Rastatt in 1714 which gave the Austrians control of Flanders. The result of which was that Philip V of Spain was allowed to remain as King of Spain but had to renounce his claim to the succession of the French throne. It was at these treaties that Spain relinquished her ownership of Gibraltar and Minorca and passed them to the English Crown. The Austrians gained Spanish territories in Italy, namely: Naples, Milan and Sardinia as well as in the Netherlands.

Jacqueline Robins: Marlborough and Prince Eugène of Austria

So to bring the story back to a more local focus Prince Eugène was joined by the British Army under the command of Lord Churchill, Duke of Marlborough. Marlborough laid siege to nearby Spanish held Aire-sur-la-Lys in 1710. The town initially withstood the considerable pressure of the attack but finally fell on November 12th 1710, not without casualties. The 10th and 18th Coldstream Guards suffered heavily during this particular campaign. With Aire-sur-la-Lys out of the way Saint-Omer was now under the spotlight.

The threat from Marlborough was very real for Saint-Omer. Times were hard for the people of France. 1709 had seen yet another famine in France and 1710 was no better. We know from a local book '*Une Année Terrible: Jacqueline Robins*' by L de Lauwereyns de Roosendaelle that 1710 was a year that '*La disette (famine), la guerre (war), les maladies (disease), désolaient à l'envi toutes nos provisions (devastated our provisions)*'. So on top of all this was the very real prospect of being wiped out by a very capable General with a highly trained and professional army. However due to the courage and bravery of a local woman Marie-Jacqueline Isabelle Robins the town was 'fortified'. She rented forty '*bélandres*', (cf Bacoves) which is a type of local boat used in Clairmarais which she used to supply the town with food and munitions. She made frequent trips to and from Saint-Omer bribing enemy sentries with eau-de-vie. A barrel of which she kept on board her bélandre. She piled her boats high with vegetables under which she concealed arms. It was a dangerous but necessary undertaking for the survival of the town. Having researched the matter locally and through the archives of the National Army Museum in London there is no record of Marlborough after all putting siege to Saint-Omer. Local opinion is divided as to how much Robins' brave endeavours did to save the town but it must have been positive enough as a statue of her by a local sculptor E Lormier was erected in 1864 in the *Place du Vainquai* commemorating her courageous deeds. Jacqueline Robins' service to the town were according to one source '*l'action d'éclat de cette femme de coeur*' or 'the brilliant actions of a lady with an enormous heart'. The statue was made of bronze and survived right up until the German occupation in 1940 when it was removed and 'never seen again'.

A heroine-like statue of Jacqueline Robins which no longer in exists. The Tower of L'Abbaye de Saint-Bertin can be clearly seen in the background. © Ms 698 Fo 6r Bibliothèque d'Agglomération de Saint-Omer

The portrait shown below is a permanent exhibit in the *Musée l'hôtel Sandelin* and the town has seen fit that her contribution to the survival of the town be celebrated in the form of the name of a road dedicated to her.

Jacqueline Isabelle Robins as seen in the Musée de l'hôtel Sandelin

© Musée de l'hôtel Sandelin

Sébastien le Prestre de Vauban (1633 – 1707)

After Louis XIV took control of Spanish Flanders he was eager to strengthen this area that historically had seen much conflict. Fortunately he had amongst his noble servant's one of the greatest military, strategic and humanist minds at his disposal – Sébastien le Prestre de Vauban. Realizing the potential that the area gave to invasion from the north and east, Vauban set about planning two lines of defence. The first line stretched from Dunkerque in the north to Maubeuge and beyond in the south east of France. This first line comprised a line of fortified towns (Dunkerque, Bergues, Furnes, Fort de Knokke, Ypres, Warneton, Menin, Lille, Tournai, Condé-sur-l'Escaut, Valanciennes, Le Quesnoy and Maubeuge). Should this line of strongly defended citadels fail, a second line of defence was formed with another chain extending from Gravelines on the coast to Avesnes-sur-Helpe in the south-east, a town about 20kms south of Maubeuge. The towns in the second line comprised Gravelines, Saint-Omer, Aire-sur-la-Lys, Saint-Venant, Béthune, Arras, Douai, Bouchain, Cambrai, Landrecies and ended at the appropriately named Avesnes-sur-Helpe, should it fail!

All the fortified towns took the form of a multi-pointed star known as the Bastion System– characteristic of Vauban's designs. Vauban's revised fortifications for Saint-Omer consisted of approximately 90 000 m2 of bricks and the creation of a mini citadel by isolating the Egmont bastion and the medieval castle. He also utilized the marshes of Clairmarais enveloping them into a defensive role for the benefit of the town. All this was rendered inadequate over time as more powerful guns were put into play. One example being the shelling of the town in 1870 by Prussian artillery positioned in Helfaut (3kms from Saint-Omer) and from the Plateau des Bruyères (the aerodrome).

Aside vast defensive walls Vauban built monumental entrances into the town. Today these rather grand but restrictive portals cease to exist. They were dismantled in the period where great modernization and restoration occurred in the 19th Century under the direction of Alexandre Ribot and Charles Jonnart.

The Religious Community just before the Revolution

One thing that is apparent even today is the number of churches that still exist in Saint-Omer. The Cathedral in all its Gothic splendour can be seen from pretty much every compass point approaching the town and before the Gothic tower of the *Abbaye de St Bertin* collapsed in 1946 that too would have been visible for miles around. It is true that Saint-Omer's reputation was once largely reliant on its Ecclesiastical importance but even so for a relatively small town it had an abundance of churches, monasteries and nunneries. You can see from the map opposite that there were the churches of *St Sépulcre, Ste Marguerite, St Jean-Baptiste, St Martin, St Denis, Ste Aldegonde,* the *Abbaye de St Bertin,* the *Cathédrale de Notre Dame,* the convents of *Ste Catherine,* the *Convent du Soleil, Les Soeurs Gris,* the Ursulines and the Poor Clares under the guidance of Mary Ward as well as in the region of 3 000 soldiers in Barracks at the *Caserne.* What an eclectic mix! However all this was about to change.

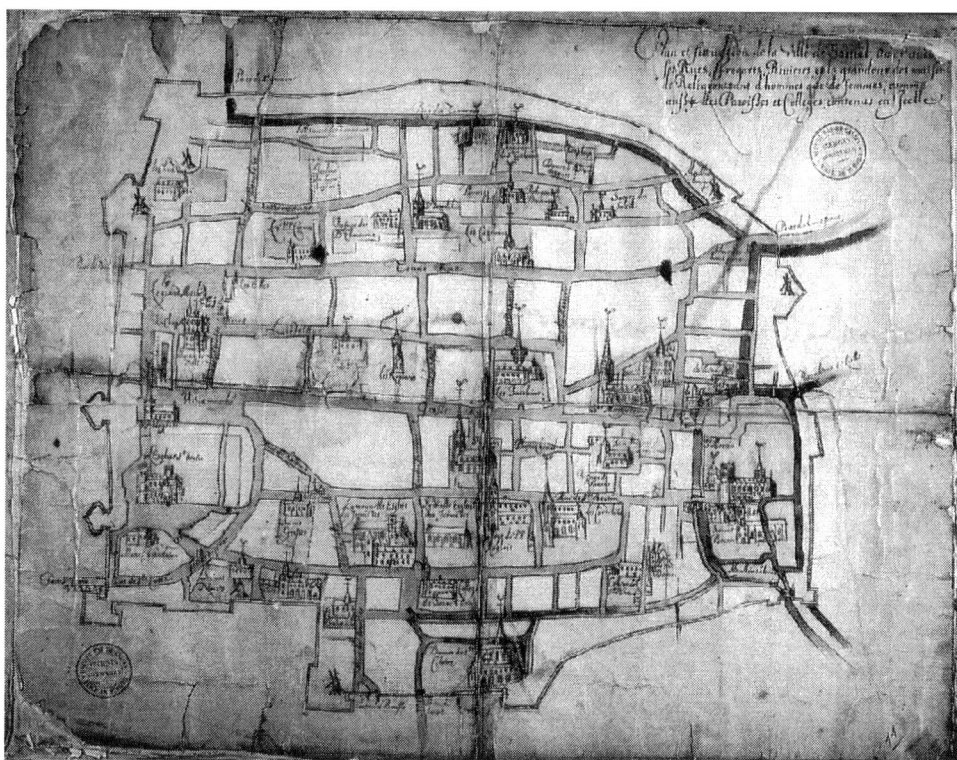

Saint-Omer's Parishes and Religious Communities in 1655
`© Ms 698 Fo 6r Bibliothèque d'Agglomération de Saint-Omer*

107

Saint Sépulcre – apparently one of only four such named churches throughout France

© Photo Jonathan Caton

The Church of Saint-Denis © Photo Jonathan Caton

Rose window of the Chapel at Lycée Sion © Photo Jonathan Caton

The French Revolution, The Terror and the biggest Brocante in history

When the Revolution started in 1789 it was law that 'anybody who did not consent to take the oath of allegiance to the civil constitution would be turned out'. Of those in the religious establishments of Saint-Omer not a single one took the oath.

The revolution for Saint-Omer brought about much change. It was 'curtains' certainly in terms of a town with significant religious clout. As we know the town was a strong and influential religious stronghold and suppression of this type of setup also occurred all over France. In Saint-Omer itself four parishes were dissolved and their churches destroyed: *Sainte Marguerite, Saint-Jean, Saint-Martin* (Now the Post Office) and *Sainte Aldegonde* (Now an open area called *Place Victor Hugo* in between the *Palais de Justice* and the *Grand Place*). Incidentally, here you can enjoy a drink at the Café de France (although not evident from the interior the façade dates from 1681 and is the oldest café in Saint-Omer) idly watching the world go by or if feeling a little more energetic try your hand at one of France's most traditional bar games: Table Football.

Saint-Omer's oldest café: Café de France © Photo Jonathan Caton

Back to the revolution and to one monastic centre in particular: *Abbaye de St Bertin*. Today, not much exists. What does remain is treasured, respected and beautifully tended. This is a far cry to the happenings after 1789. The oil painting below by Lemaire shows the extent of the Abbey and its community.

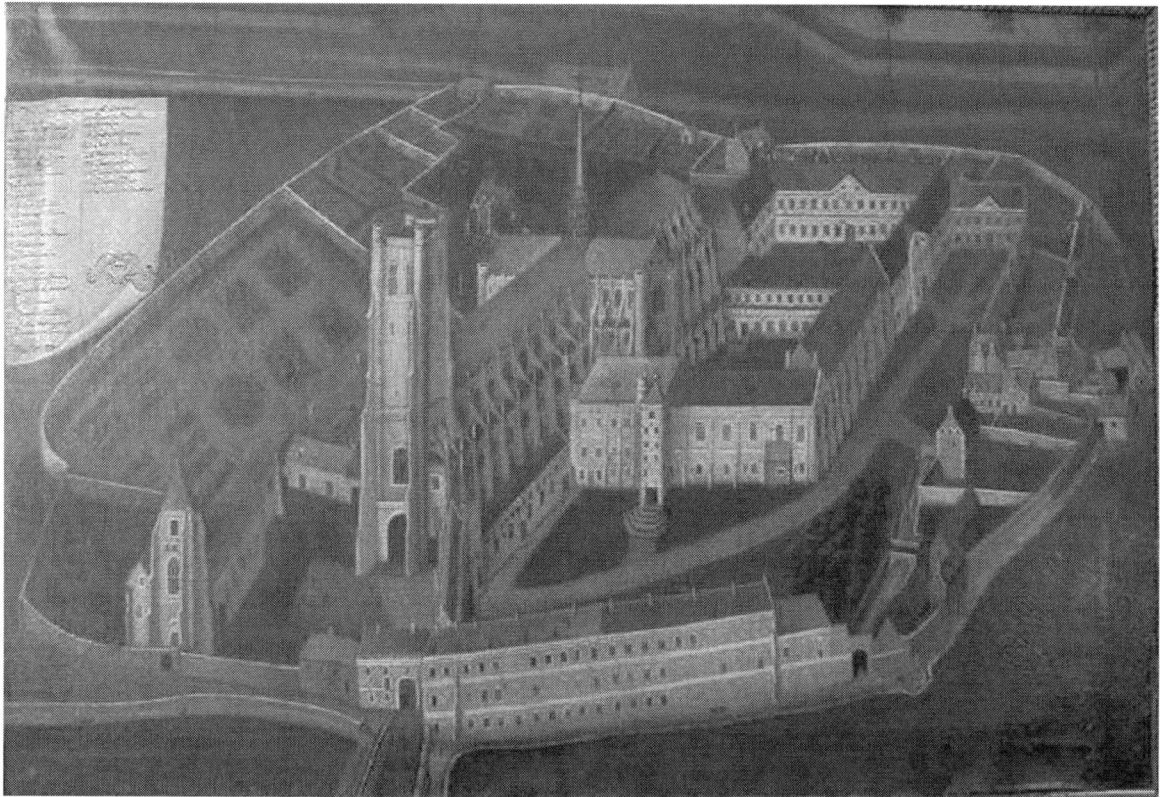

Abbaye St Bertin as it was before the revolution by Lemaire. This picture is on permanent display in Musée de l'hôtel Sandelin © Musée de l'hôtel Sandelin

With its formidable reputation as a centre of religion The Abbey earned over time huge respect and played host to many visiting dignitaries and events. The rather fearsome statue of Abbot Suger that you see looking over the car park in front of the Abbey is testament to the early power of the establishment.

Abbot Suger outside the ruins of the Abbaye de St Bertin
© Société Académique des Antiquaires de la Morinie

You will notice that Suger's mitre and sceptre have been placed on the floor next to him whilst Suger himself is posing as if a Roman Senator resting his elbow on top of a crown – this stance reflects his position as Regent of France. It also represents the influence that he had in the courts where he was both friend and counsel to Louis VI

(1081 – 1137) and Louis VII (1120 – 1180). Suger, according to some sources was a native of Saint-Omer and was a revered historian and author of many books. Suger was also very interested in architecture. It was he who was instrumental in the rebuilding of the first Gothic church in France - St Denis in Paris. He was a great collector particularly of works from the craftsmen and artisans of Liège.

The rather foreboding statue that you see in the square in front of the west door of the ruined Abbey carries an interesting story. Back in 1878 the town was given the chance of obtaining a statue of Abbot Suger by the acclaimed sculptor Louis Noël to put in front of the abandoned Abbey. Examples of Noël's work can be seen in *Place Sithieu* with his bronze sculpture of the musician Pierre Alexandre de   Monsigny, also at the *Cimetière des Bruyères* in the form of the bust of the French Senator Edouard Devaux and also in the *Palais de Justice* – formerly Archbishop's House near the Cathedral.

French Senator Edouard Devaux as sculpted by Louis Noël as seen at the Cimetière des Bruyères© Photo Jonathan Caton.

Everyone was very excited about this until the estimated bill arrived. The sum demanded was too great for the town to pay so the project was shelved. Many years later, in fact in 1939, the Palace of Versailles had a statue of Suger in one of their courtyards and they were searching for a new home for him so they offered the twelve ton stone figure as a gift to the town on the proviso that he was collected. The offer was readily accepted and hence Saint-Omer now has Abbot Suger formerly of the Palace of Versailles!

Abbot Suger being transported to Saint-Omer from Versailles
© Société Académique des Antiquaires de la Morinie

The *Abbaye* was not dissolved immediately. Initially the Revolutionary government sent Bishop Porion, a renegade, to take charge in April 1791. He had rules of his own, dictating 'administration' but also bending rules on his religious position, for instance deciding to get married despite being a Roman Catholic Bishop. In another source Porion is exposed as acting as a contractor and furnishing stores to the army.

Joining Porion was a certain curé or priest called Michaud. Allegedly he dispensed with some of the monks and put the church to his own uses. The last remaining monks (of which there were forty) were kicked out of *Saint-Bertin* in August 1791. Allegedly Michaud pulled down the 'rood' screen, and built himself a baptistery. Evidence of this addition was apparent right up until 1946 when the ruins suffered their final injury with the tower collapsing due to bomb damage from a raid in 1944. Michaud's undoing was not because of his unique method of conducting either the Abbaye's administrative affairs or his self-approved building programmes but for his refusal to surrender the bells. Saint-Omer is famous for its bells and remains so today. As a result he was sent to the scaffold. Surely a perfect example of don't ask who the bells toll for, they toll for me!

However none of this altered the inevitable and soon after *l'Abbaye de St Bertin* was dissolved. The mother church of Saint-Omer which had been operational since the seventh century was now defunct.

The *Abbaye's* demise was not conducted over a number of weeks but years. Between 1791 and the end of 1792 the contents, amongst them the organ were sold off. The Abbaye and other buildings on the site were sold on 17th March 1799 for demolition with the exception of the Tower which was to be kept as a watch tower. However it was not until July 1811 that all that remained of the *Abbaye* was acquired by the town of Saint-Omer. The vast collections of books from the monastic libraries which had made this part of France famous throughout Europe were sold off as each religious community was snuffed out. Hundreds of year's worth of work and investment all gone in about twenty four months. It is estimated that during this period in the region of five million books of incalculable value 'disappeared', many never to be seen again. In terms of lost culture and knowledge it was a culling of stupefying proportions. This of course pales into insignificance when one considers the forty thousand 'guillotinings' that occurred during the Reign of Terror (1793-1794). The *Bibliothèque of Saint-Omer* has preserved a considerable number of books taken from St Bertin's libraries amongst others. If you have time to visit the *Salle du Patrimoine* at the Library of Saint-Omer please note the panelling in this room. It is the original taken from the library of the *Abbaye de St Bertin*.

The Salle du Patrimoine at the Bibliothèque de Saint-Omer © Bibliothèque de Saint-Omer

Everything was treated ruthlessly. All the chalices, silver plate, rich with precious stones were piled into a heap and sold to passing traders. Six of the seven bells were melted down for cannons or coins. The Musée de *l'hôtel Sandelin* displays many of the smaller relics from the *Abbaye* amongst them being carvings in stone of angels with a scroll or small sculptures done in ivory, statuettes of many of the Saints, chalices and paintings such as *Notre Dame de Milan*. Parts of the tops of the shutters from the main altarpiece can be seen in The National Gallery in London. Other panels from this famous altar can be seen in Berlin.

Much of the religious furniture, fixtures and fittings inside the Abbaye and other churches were sold off or acquired; taken for example to the pretty village of Tournehem-sur-la-Hem and its church of *Saint Médard* (12kms north of Saint-Omer) which has some magnificent pieces including the pews originating from some of the larger churches located in or near Saint-Omer.

119

You don't have to leave Saint-Omer to see the splendour that once was the great *Abbaye de St Bertin*. You need only go to the Cathedral and look at the large ornate golden altar with its six enormous gold candlesticks soaring skyward on the high altar. And built into this impressive piece of church furniture are some relics of St Bertin himself.

The main altar at the Cathedral once a focal point in L'Abbaye de St Bertin
© Photo Jonathan Caton

Pieces from the *Abbaye* are now dispersed all over the world but curiously enough some of the fine hand painted stained glass windows found their way to England in 1828 and are now in Shiplake Church, Shipley near Oxford.

Shiplake Church - home to some of the stained glass originating from the Abbaye de Saint Bertin © Société Académique des Antiquaires de la Morinie

Details of the stained glass windows originating from the Abbaye de St Bertin. Please note the double cross seen in the central window © Société Académique des Antiquaires de la Morinie

As one can see from the etching below the ruins, although by this time roofless, would have provided quite an impressive spectacle. So much so that Charles X of France and his son, the Duke of Angoulême, came to visit them in 1827 whilst staying at the *hôtel Sandelin*.

RUINES DE L'ÉGLISE DU STE BERTIN. (Année 1844)
Vue extérieure et générale prise en ouest

The ruins as seen in 1814 by Emmanuel Wallet, engraving
© *Ms 698 Fo 6r Bibliothèque d'Agglomération de Saint-Omer*

In 1830 the demolition continued in earnest. Development plans had been drawn up and it was agreed that those people out of work or as the French say *'chômeurs'* were gainfully employed in dismantling much of the *Abbaye* to recuperate the stone for other municipal projects. The stone was used to build the affectionately known "coffee-mill" *Hôtel de Ville* with its magnificent but sadly un-used gem of a little Italianate theatre. This fine neoclassical building is the work of Pierre-Bernard Lefranc, as is the rather splendid *Salle de Concert* seen overleaf.

Hôtel de Ville and Salle de Concert – a marvellous concert hall and one of the oldest Music Schools in France. Both by Pierre-Bernard Lefranc 1834 ©Photo Jonathan Caton

An English settlement sprang up around the ruins about 1825 after a certain Caroline Degacher (wife of a George Henry Horn) bought a house in the St Bertin enclos for four thousand francs, the purpose of which was to set up a boarding school. Soon a small community of English natives lived round about, among them a Doctor called Edward Whitfield, an Anglican Reverend called Wilkinson and an ex-army Officer called Rodney Brighton. The colony gradually disappeared after the school was sold to Walter Hitchcock in 1844 for reasons unknown. (18).The intellectual powerhouse that was the Jesuit College was suppressed and the movement fled to Bruges in Belgium.

After The Revolution the whole of France was divided up into 98 departments which comprised of arrondissements, cantons and communes. The Pas-de-Calais is the 62nd department (You can easily identify the locals by the number 62 that appears on car number plates). 62 was then divided into 6 arrondissements which in turn were split into 86 cantons and finally apportioned into 935 communes. The arrondissements of 62 were at the time Arras, Béthune, Boulogne, Montreuil, Saint-Omer and Saint-Pol.

In order of size Saint-Omer was second only to Arras. Saint-Omer had 15 cantons and 137 communes. Today little has changed in terms of arrondissement classification, except that Saint-Pol is no longer categorized as such and Calais has been added.

The special blend of tobacco from Saint-Omer

Saint-Omer still had many commercial interests despite its religious guillotining. Pipes and all things relating to the smoking of tobacco were one of them and were produced here as well as a rather beautiful and sought-after style of porcelain.

As we know, tobacco was brought over from America by Christopher Columbus around 1492 and in 1561 the appropriately named Scholar and Diplomat Jean Nicot (1530 – 1600) brought the plant to France via the court of Catherine de Medicis who was a big fan of the latest fad. As a result in 1630 Clairmarais started to grow tobacco with great success. The first manufacturer was established in 1660 and the rate of growth was rapid. In 1750 there were seventeen producers which had increased to twenty-eight by 1789, employing 450 people. As a former martyr to the weed I was interested as to the particular tobacco types grown here. I can only hazard a guess but two varieties might have been 'Dark Air-Cured Tobacco' which once cured was very dark in colour as the name implies giving off a strong cigar-like perfume and also '*Perique*' which was left to mature for up to ten months giving off rich prune-like and aromatic wisps of not unpleasant scented curls.

But the big question was: what to smoke it in? This question will be answered admirably with a visit to Musée de l'hôtel Sandelin. Here some two thousand pipes of amazing originality and some of exquisite finesse are displayed in a clear, uncluttered and interesting way. Most of them were given to the museum by the widow of the last pipe manufacturer in Saint-Omer, Madame Emile Duméril. The vast majority of those on display show that it really was a fashion mainly for the wealthy and the well to do. So around this vibrant business appeared two of the most distinguished Pipe Makers in France if not Europe. They are Fiolet of Saint-Omer who was in business from 1765 to 1921 and Duméril - Leurs from 1845 – 1885, again from Saint-Omer.

The themes for these pipes are highly imaginative, strikingly colourful and beautifully executed. Many of them have an animal theme such as an elephant with a long extended trunk, there are monkeys, crickets, soldiers, pipes with Italianate scenes on them and obviously more than the occasional *risqué* one.

The pipe and tobacco industry flourished for about 130 years before its decline with the arrival of cigars and cigarettes. The last factory closed around 1909. It is interesting to note that one of the school buildings of *the College de Saint-Bertin* situated *in rue St Bertin* was originally the home of Louis Alexandre Fiolet.

The fine townhouse originally belonging to Louis Alexandre Fiolet of the Pipe production world
© Photo Jonathan Caton

The interior of the building still shows the elegance of the time in particular the sweeping staircase, stucco mouldings and wood patterned floors.

One of the great gems of the North – L'hôtel Sandelin

It is now an appropriate moment to introduce one of the architectural and cultural gems of the town and indeed northern France – Musée de l'hôtel Sandelin.

Front façade and Courtyard of Hôtel Sandelin - Originally the winter residence for the Countess of Fruges and since 1904 Musée Sandelin © Photo Jonathan Caton

The building was originally the winter home of Marie-Josèphe Sandelin - Countess of Fruges. Little is known of the Sandelin family except that the Countess was of dual nationality; French and Spanish. Obviously for an aristocratic family, the building was designed in true Parisian style using Marquise stone. The addition of the word 'hôtel' in the name of the building does not have anything to do with paying guests, mini-bars or porters. *'Hôtel'* was a common way or rather an aristocratic way of saying my 'large' house which would more accurately translate as 'mansion'. The building boasts an impressive courtyard large enough to accommodate arriving and departing carriages with landscaped gardens to the rear. The front courtyard which once had a grand fountain as a central feature is flanked by what were stables which are typical of the French Louis XV and Louis XVI periods.

The building was constructed in incredibly quick time even by modern standards 1775 – 1777. Initially intended as the residence for both the Duchess Marie-Josèphe and her husband Pierre Sandelin, the Duchess came to live in the hôtel a widow. Pierre died in 1776. It was in fact a number of years after the building was completed that Marie-Josèphe was able to face living here. As obvious targets during the Revolution the Duchess fled France with her brother to Spain (Barcelona). During this period the hôtel was requisitioned by the newly formed Administration, becoming its headquarters between 1795 – 1803 and then the sub-Prefecture up to 1808. As for the contents these were sold off between 1794-1795. After 1808 the Sandelin family successfully negotiated the return of their home and Marie-Josèphe returned there in 1808 only to die a few weeks later on the 20 April 1808 at the then ripe old age of 75. The Hôtel stayed in the possession of the family until 1899 when the building was sold to the town. In 1904 after careful planning and negotiation by the then Sénateur-Maire François Ringot the town of Saint-Omer had in its cultural arsenal a fabulous venue for a museum.

Today it is a splendid museum. On display there are a huge array of fascinating artefacts, pictures, tapestries, porcelain, furniture, religious art, swords, firearms, model soldiers and tobacco pipes. I use the word splendid as the truly apt adjective to describe the museum itself. The exhibits are arranged in an ordered and beautifully presented way. The concept of the interior is from a team of three well known architects Petr Opelik, Frédérique Paoletti and Catherine Rouland. Leading the project was Petr Opelik who graduated from Prague in 1981 and then L'Ecole Paris la Villette in 1985 and has since gone on to redesign the Theatre Kursaal in Bully-les-Mines in addition to Musée Sandelin in 2004. Frederique Paoletti and Catherine Rouland have since been involved in the construction of other major European projects including museums in Paris, Cherbourg, Mulhouse and Le Musée du Tumulus de Bougon. Most of the museum is given over to exhibition space and it certainly warrants a couple of hours of your time or even several separate visits. The majority of the rooms on the ground floor have been restored to their former glory and are as they would have been first seen and approved by the Countess. The building is classed as a *Monument Historique*. The walls are adorned with masterpieces dating from the 11th - 19th centuries by renowned international artists as well as home grown ones such as Léon Belly (Saint-Omer 1827 – Paris 1877). Another, Louis-Léopold Boilly (La Bassée 1761 – Paris 1845) who was a gifted satirist in the same mould as Hogarth, leaves us a series of four pictures depicting the story of the deceived lover. They continue to amaze in their intricate detail of objects and expression. Many of his works are on permanent display in the Wallace Collection in London.

Then there is the rather horrible depiction of medieval medical practice in action by Breugel the Elder (Brueghel c.1528 – Brussels 1569) in his painting entitled *The Excision of the Stone of Madness.*

There is a fine example of the Queen of all Mistresses of a certain *époque*, that being Jeanne Antoinette Poisson who by alluring the French king with her beauty quickly shed her surname of Miss Fish for the much grander Madame de Pompadour (1721 – 1764), *maîtresse-en-titre* to Louis XV. Painted many times during her royal lifetime the example that Sandelin has is by a Parisian artist of some renown - Jean-Marc Nattier (Paris 1685 – Paris 1766).

From further a-field there is a picture by the fiery tempered Michelangelo da Caravaggio (1573 near Milan – Porto Ercole 1610) called *The Disciples of Emmaüs.*

The Disciples of Emmaus attributed to Michelangelo Merisi Caravaggio. This picture is a copy of a picture found in the Our Lady's Church in Bruges. © Musée de l'hôtel Sandelin

Portrait of Madame de Pompadour en Diane by Jean-Marc Nattier painted in 1748.

Oil on canvas. © Musée de l'hôtel Sandelin

There are many works from artists originating from Saint-Omer amongst them being Léon Belly (Saint-Omer 1826 – Paris 1871), Abel Bertram (Saint-Omer 1871 – Paris 1954), Auguste Bugat (Saint-Omer 1843 – Saint-Omer 1912), François Chifflart (Saint-Omer 1825 – Paris 1901), Hippolyte Cuvelier (Saint-Omer c.1803 – 1876), Marie-Madeleine Descelers (Saint-Omer 1897 – Saint-Omer 1964), Jules Génisson (Saint-Omer 1805 – Bruges 1860), Henri Charles Hancquier (Saint-Omer 1821 – Saint-Omer 1883), Jules Joets (Saint-Omer 1884 – Viry-Châtillon 1959), Alphonse de Neuville (Saint-Omer 1835 – Paris 1885), Omer Pley (Saint-Omer 1803 – Saint-Omer 1897) and Louis Villeneuve (Saint-Omer 1813 – Saint-Omer 1881).

Many of the streets close to *Musée Sandelin* are in fact named after these artists one example being the *Ecole des Beaux Arts* which is situated in *rue Alphonse de Neuville*.

Alphonse de Neuville in his studio taken from the Journal Les Annales Politiques et littéraires No 336 1889 © Ms 698 Fo 6r Bibliothèque d'Agglomération de Saint-Omer

One of De Neuville's pictures that hangs in Sandelin is his *Siège de Sebastopol*. This impressive canvas depicts the siege (1854-1855) which led to the defeat of Russia in the Crimean War. The siege lasted a year resulting in a horrendous number of casualties from all sides involved, namely: Britain, France, Turkey and their opponent Russia. The siege helped bring about huge changes in the medical services of both Britain and Russia through the tireless work of Florence Nightingale and Nikolai Piragov respectively. Changes also came about as a result of this most bloody war in Britain's effort to recognise the highest feats of bravery from its servicemen, thus came the ultimate British Military Honour – The Victoria Cross. The base metal is poor quality but nevertheless originates from Russian owned, but not necessarily made, 18 pounder guns that were captured at the siege.

Not surprisingly, given Saint-Omer's religious heritage, Sandelin possesses many highly prized exhibits of a religious nature. Some we have already been introduced to, but two that shine out (to me) are by the famed Florentine ceramic sculptor Andrea Della Robbia (1435 – 1525). A master craftsman of lead glazed terracotta. His works are mainly in Italy especially in his own area of Tuscany at the Borgello Palace in Florence or at Pistoia Cathedral for example, but you don't have to go all the way to Italy to see examples of his work. The works in question are La Mort et l'Epitaple Death and Epitaph and Le Prophète Jérémie. Curiously enough there is another example of his work called The Annunciation in the nearby church of St-Martin-au-Laërt (pronounced 'Lar') which once adorned the tomb of a former Bishop of Saint-Bertin Guillaume Fillastre.

The basement exhibits artefacts from the ruined Cathedral at Thérouanne, swords, masonry and Flemish sculptures from the former Hôtel de Ville whilst the first floor offers the fabulous collection of pipes that we have already discussed and an enviable collection of porcelain from all over the globe including examples from some of the world's greatest - Delft, Lille, Strasbourg, Nevers and of course Saint-Omer.

Porcelain production in Saint-Omer came about as a result of a patent issued to two potters: Louis Saladin from Dunkerque and Adrien Levesque from Rouen authorising them to open a faience factory in the Haut-Pont area of the town. Saint-Omer was their preferred choice because of its excellent trading connections, its proximity to the sea as well as the quality of the clay and an abundant supply of wood for the firing process. The decree for their proposed factory was sent to the council and was registered on July 9th 1751. Amongst small trading details the potters were authorised to manufacture over a period of twenty years a "faience in the style of Holland, fit to stand the fire, and crockery in stoneware in the English style." Some designs are obviously inspired by Saint-Omer's surrounding Clairmarais. Insects and birds feature a lot in the designs as well as more adventurous creations such as soup tureens moulded as cabbages and wild boar!

The Boar's Head. A once common site charging through the woods of Clairmarais – by this I mean the whole boar not just the head. © Musée de l'hôtel Sandelin

There are over 3000 exhibits to see in this wonderful museum and it is worth visiting. It is also worthwhile noting that there are occasional evening concerts in the summer which can be enjoyed in the gardens with a glass of wine in addition to a variety of interesting activities to participate in during the '*Journées du Patrimoine*' (Heritage Days when most museums across France are free) every September.

Returning to our history and its curious Britannic connections there was one notable English visitor to the town in 1783: Horatio Nelson. He arrived in the town on Tuesday 28th October with the intention of learning French. He was 25 years old and he came with a friend of his called James MacNamara who had been a fellow Lieutenant on HMS Bristol in 1778. Letters show that they both enjoyed their stay taking tea and playing cards well into the night. The exact location of where they stayed is not known save that it is in the area of *rue Hendricq*. (19)

Saint-Omer Rulers: French	First Republic up to 1804
	Napoléon 1er (Bonaparte) 1804 - 1815
	Second Republic 1848 – 1852
	Second Empire 1852 - 1870
	Third Republic 1870 – 1940
Throne of Great Britain & Northern Ireland	George III (b.1738) k.fr: 1760 – 1820
	George IV (b.1762) k.fr: 1820 - 1830
	William IV (b.1765) k.fr: 1830 – 1837
	Victoria (b.1819) qu.fr: 1837 – 1901

KEY DATES

1801	English crown stops inference to being Ruler of France and England
1803	A quarter of Napoléon Bonaparte's Army of England barracked in Saint-Omer
1805	British navy defeats the Franco-Spanish fleet at the Battle of Trafalgar under the command of Admiral Horatio Nelson
1812	Distillerie de Houlle opens for business
1815	Napoléon defeated at the Battle of Waterloo
1825	La Verrerie Cristallerie d'Arques opens – forerunner of ARC International
1828	Shiplake church in Oxfordshire acquires windows from l'Abbaye de St-Bertin
1830	Materials, fixtures and fittings of l'Abbaye de St Bertin sold off to the displeasure of many, among them being Victor Hugo
1834	The Hôtel de Ville of Saint-Omer styled on a wing from Palais of Versailles starts to be built – using stone quarried from l'Abbaye de St Bertin
1848	Saint-Omer is connected to the rail network

Although the town itself was not touched by heavy industry the area around it saw considerable developments during the 19th Century and amongst others was the opening of one of the last surviving gin distilleries in France. But more on this interesting topic later. First off Britain has to face up to the prospect of invasion. This time not by a Norman but by the most famous Corsican of all: Napoléon Bonaparte.

Saint-Omer, Napoléon Bonaparte and the Army of England

The French troops billeted in Saint-Omer in 1803 were just too early to benefit from the restorative qualities of the gin produced at the distillery at Houlle. The Army of England was one of Napoléon's Grand plans and it consisted of four armies based at Utrecht, Bruges, Montreuil and Saint-Omer at the Plateau des Bruyères (20). This is where the aerodrome is situated today. The ports required for this vast flotilla of row boats were to be located at Boulogne-sur-Mer and Etaples. In 1803 up to twenty thousand troops and artillery were stationed here and in the barracks in the town under the command of Marshal Soult, a most trusted General and held in high regard by Napoléon.

Soult was nicknamed by his own troops as the 'Hand of Iron' and by his English adversaries as the 'Duke of Damnation'. He had a high regard for the English Infantry whom he described in combat as being like the Devil *'en duel c'est le diable!'*. As commander of Napoléon's army of the North he fought against the British at Waterloo in 1815.

As history shows us the invasion plan was somewhat flawed partly by Napoléon's refusal to acknowledge the power of the British Royal Navy and its successful blockade of French ports but also in the proposed method of transporting such a huge army across a very unpredictable stretch of water.

There were fantastic plans for immense hot air balloons with flatbed platforms capable of carrying whole cavalry and artillery regiments and most ambitious of all the ideas was of digging a channel tunnel. However a more practical method was pursued in the form of boats. Napoléon was a stickler for attention to detail and he wrote to Marshal Soult cataloguing the strict training programme. He declared that all the soldiers in the boats were to learn to swim (21) – presumably for those stationed in Saint-Omer this would have meant Clairmarais!

It is worth just explaining a little more about these boats. There were four types ranging from the largest known as the Prame which was flat-bottomed affair about 100 feet long – some had small cannons as protection. The smallest vessels were known as 'péniches'. A point of interest is that 'péniche' is the name for a canal barge in modern French. These are deckless affairs of about 60ft by 10ft and manned by a crew of five sailors. They have a capacity for carrying fifty-five soldiers who provide the power by rowing. The calm waters of Clairmarais were just about the limit of stability for this type of boat. In choppier water the soldiers' newly acquired swimming skills would most definitely be called for. Napoléon was banking on an absolutely flat Channel on which his 2000 *péniches* could safely cross.

Napoléon sent twenty three precise instructions to Soult regarding rowing technique that he wanted from 'Command One: Embark!' Below is an example of these precise instructions for 'Command Six: Row'

"At this command every man holding the butt of the oars stretches forward together; they lean on the butt so that the blade does not plunge into the water until they have fully extended their arms. When their arms are stretched right forward, they let the butt of the oar rise gradually so as to plunge the blade some seven inches into the water, and at the same time they draw the oar to the rear by pulling hard on the butt. Note: In order that the péniche be rowed well, it is essential that the two oarsmen on the near most bench row together and in well marked rhythm..."

Despite the failure of his navy to rendezvous near Boulogne as planned on account of being dispersed by the Royal Navy, Napoléon remained supremely confident in the success of his invasion of England. So much so that he remarked on 16th November 1803 "that the Channel was just a ditch which will be leaped whenever one has the boldness to try". He motivated Admiral Ganteaume with these words: 'I count on your talents, your steadfastness and your character. Put to sea and sail here. We will avenge six centuries of insults and shame. Never have any soldiers on land and sea risked their lives for so great an object." Two days later Napoléon ordered Soult and his other Generals to pack up and get ready for a long march east. Due to Nelson's victory over the Franco-Spanish fleet at Trafalgar on 21st October 1805 and the displacement of the fleet designated to help escort Napoléon's flotilla across the Channel the grand plan for the invasion of England was consigned permanently to history's bin.

Napoléon Bonaparte (French Invasion or Bonaparte landing in Great Britain) by James Gillray, published by Hannah Humphrey hand-coloured etching, published 10 June 1803

© National Portrait Gallery, London

So onward to the cognac of the North: Genièvre or Gin to you and me

Gin production in the 18th Century in northern France and Flanders was big business - legal or otherwise. It was introduced to England by soldiers returning from campaigns in the Low Countries from the 1740's onwards. It made smugglers rich on account of the high taxation placed on it —not so dissimilar to the modern 'booze cruises' of the 1980's. As relations between France and Britain deteriorated Napoléon declared a trade boycott with Britain; this however did not include gin production as he found he was able to use the frequent visits by smugglers to ferry his spies backwards and forwards across the Channel as well as in a small way deny valuable taxation to the British Government. The pickup points for smugglers were the beaches of Gravelines. In 1810 there were seventy-two registered gin distilleries operating in France. Two hundred years on only three remain; Houlle, Loos and Wambrechies. The *Distillerie Persyn* at Houlle has been in and out of various branches of the same family since its creation in 1812 and for those of us who might be a bit shady on the history side of things that means it was bottling when the Iron Duke Wellington was grappling with Napoléon up at not so far away 'Waterloo' in Belgium. The current owners are the Persyn Family who have been in ownership and guardians of the artisan techniques since 1944. Little has changed in terms of method and quality.

The Distillery at Houlle © Photo Jonathan Caton

The distillery occupies a tranquil site along the banks of the River Houlle, as it has since its creation. Passion is the driving force of this *'genièvre'* as it is known in French. As with all artisan products of excellence, quality not quantity is key. The rolling hills of the Pas-de-Calais provide all the climatic conditions necessary to give top quality raw ingredients namely, sun (don't laugh we do get it from *temps-en-temps*!), rain (yes we get a lot of that!), wind and sea breezes – all giving their own unique touch to the base components: oats, barley and rye. The idea of *'terroir'* is not just for vignerons and wine connoisseurs.

Mass production is not part of the Persyn business plan. Producing a relatively small 300 hectolitres of *genièvre* per year, that's about 60 000 bottles, *Genièvre de Houlle* prides itself on its blending which, like malt whiskies, relies on the skill of the blender. Here technique gives way to nose and experience.

The initial blending of oats, barley and rye is done by hand and with nothing more sophisticated than a shovel. This sounds very basic but the differing amounts of the core ingredients differ depending on what the blender is trying to achieve. This mixture is then ground and turned into a flour like substance. I am not going to go into the technicalities too much; suffice to say I will be hopefully clear and brief. After all it is the final *'dégustation'* that one finds most interesting.

The 'flour' is added to very hot water – between 70-100 degrees Celsius. This mixture is described as cereal starch and is allowed to cool to exactly 30 degrees. The liquid is now transferred to fermentation vats where nature is allowed to take its course and the starch turns into sugar. Yeast is now added to create fermented malt. This fermentation period takes three days.

The Persyn stills are antique, copper, well used and look it. They are both well over a hundred years old and are now fired by *'gaz-de-ville'* as opposed to wood. There are three stages of distillation taking between thirty-two and thirty-six hours to complete. The first round of distillation produces a brew of around 18 degrees of alcohol – this increases over the next two stages to finish at around 55 degrees. It is during the third and final distillation that the 'juniper' fusion is utilised. The brew is allowed to pass through the juniper berries by way of condensation, thus extracting in the subtlest way the medicinal qualities (it was considered thus once upon a time) and aromatic flavours of these exotic berries. The alcohol is merely touched by the flavour – not immersed in it.

The genièvre is now ready for barrelling. The Persyn barrels are a *mélange* of old and new - all oak. Barrel age is very important – young barrels add a more caramelised colour and possibly the slight harshness of youth, which is not as subtle as the older generation. Maturation can be months or years depending on the blenders' final choice of required flavour and style.

And now for the tasting! I was given two to try, The Special (43%) and the Carte Dorée (40%). Both were served in chilled brandy style glasses (about 10 degrees). I tried the Special first. The nose is apparent straight off. You can really smell the cereals used. Now this is not so surprising because the unique character of the Special is that at the first stage of production more oats are added into the original cereal mix. It is not an over-powering smell, it is a homely smell, strong in alcohol but with a nice roundness. The colour is comparable to a young white wine, pale and slightly golden. The 'Special' has a thickish quality not too dissimilar to a liqueur in fact it is often drunk as a *'digestif'* after a meal. The Carte Dorée variety has a strong presence of cereals on the nose but was lighter in style and colour. Again the taste was subtly round and most excellent served on its own with or without ice. There are several other varieties available, a 'prestige' bottle called Carte Noire (49%), La Foscade (45%) which is usually used as a base for cocktails or with tonic and a rich whisky coloured variety called 'Brut de Fûts' which has been matured for five years and has not been blended – so in essence a single malt gin!

The *genièvre* comes in either glass or ceramic bottles (50cl or 70cl) the latter being the traditional style of bottle used in the 1800's because gin is best served chilled so in the absence of fridges chilling had to be done by lowering supplies into water wells!

Returning to our historical journey we now face the Franco-Prussian War. The result of which was hugely important to France in general and for Saint-Omer as a frontier town housing a large garrison it was significant.

The results of the Franco-Prussian war were humiliating for France, resulting in two inglorious defeats. The first at Metz (August – October 1870), the second at the battle of Sedan (September 1870) at the hands of the Prussians which led to the Siege of Paris (September 1870 – January 1871). The Siege of Paris left the inhabitants so desperate that rats, dogs and cats were eaten to feed themselves. The menu opposite shows the extent to which Parisians were forced to stoop in a bid for survival.

In addition to this the terms of the Treaty of Frankfurt were ignominious. As a result of the Treaty the French were forced to concede Alsace, Lorraine and much of the Vosges areas of France. In addition French citizens residing in Alsace-Lorraine were given until October 1872 to decide whether they wanted to remain French or become German citizens. If the former was chosen it meant moving from the area. A huge sum of 5 billion francs was also demanded and paid to the Prussians within three years of the Treaty. Feelings of 'revenge' would help carry France eagerly into the horrors of the First World War.

For Saint-Omer military change came about as a result of this war. The garrison town was upgraded to 2nd Class. The area was very important militarily and was considered as 'frontline'. Saint-Omer along with Aire-sur-la-Lys (62), Bergues (59), Boulogne-sur-Mer (62), Calais (62), Cassel (59), Dunkerque (59), Gravelines (59) and Hesdin (62) were the garrison towns of the departments 62 and 59.(22)

The following regiments were garrisoned in Saint-Omer at this time:

At the *Caserne d'Esplanade* was the *Bataillon de Chasseurs à Pied* (French Light Infantry) and depot for the *17ème Bataillon C.P.* This is now called the *Esplanade* and is where you can park for free all day with excellent access to the centre of town by foot except Saturday mornings when, if you are not early the market traders take the lot! The *Caserne de Cygne* (now the car park nearest to *Place Victor Hugo*) was the depot for the *6ème Bataillon C.P.*and the *Caserne de Cavalerie: 1er Régiment du Train Artillerie.*

MENU

25 Décembre 1870

99ᵐᵉ Jour du Siège

Hors-d'Œuvre :

Beurre, Radis, Tête d'Ane Farcie, Sardines

Potages :

Purée de Haricots rouges aux Croûtons
Consommé d'Éléphant

Entrées :

Goujons frits. - Le Chameau rôti à l'anglaise
Le Civet de Kangourou
Côtes d'Ours rôties sauce Poivrade

Rôts :

Cuissot de Loup, sauce Chevreuil
Le Chat flanqué de Rats
Salade de Cresson
La Terrine d'Antilope aux truffes
Cèpes à la Bordelaise
Petits-Pois au Beurre

Entremets :

Gâteau de riz aux Confitures

Dessert :

Fromage de Gruyère

VINS

1ᶜʳ Service	2ᵐᵉ Service
Xérès	Mouton Rothschild 1846
	Romanée Conti 1858
Latour Blanche 1861	Bellenger frappé
Ch. Palmer 1864	Grand Porto 1827

Café & Liqueurs

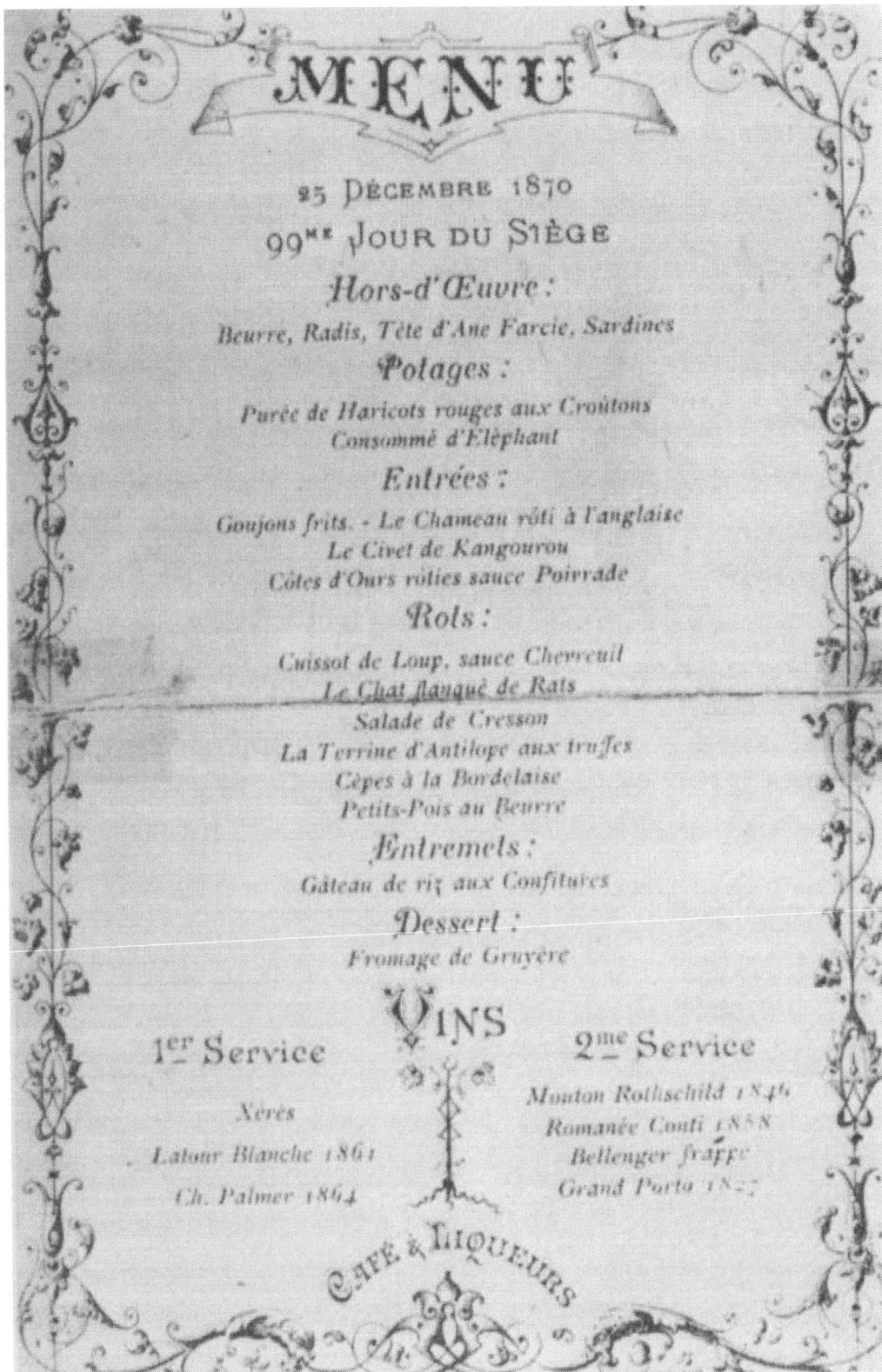

A Christmas Day Menu with a considerable difference as shown by this
Parisian Restaurant during the height of the Siege of 1870-1

There are many buildings in Saint-Omer that reveal the town's military heritage. The picture below shows one of the most prominent – *La Caserne de La Barre.*

La Caserne de La Barre © Photo Jonathan Caton

Today the interior has been developed into very desirable flats but the building dates back to 1685 when it became the Officers Quarters. We know that in 1701 it was home to around 780 officers.

Up to 1914 regiments came and went, some staying longer periods than others. It is however worth noting that these regiments were some of the finest in the French Army. An example being the *8ème R.I.* which was barracked here from 1875 to 1920. As we shall see they suffered heavy losses during the First World War and judging by the following recorded event took a fair battering during the Franco-Prussian War. We are told that on the 18th June 1895 a magnificent military Tattoo took place in the town. The inspection of the troops was led by *'Le Général de France'*, Head of the *1er Corps d'Armée* who had come to honour the 8th Infantry Regiment by presenting them with a new flag. In his speech to the assembled troops he proudly proclaimed:

"*Un jour viendra, peut-être, ou, pour venger de cruelles défaites (by that he meant the defeat of the French in the Franco-Prussian War of 1870), vous devrez, à votre tour, marcher au combat. Ayez alors la volonté de vaincre, et l'Histoire enregistrera sur votre drapeau de nouvelles victoires, car, le voulant, vous serez invincible*". (23). The gist being that one day, perhaps a day would come when the 8th could avenge their cruel defeat suffered at the hands of the Prussians and they would be able to record their victories on their new flag.

However there was no '*peut-être*' about it. For around the corner – historically speaking – came arguably the most unnecessary, costly in every sense of the word and appalling conflicts of all time: World War One.

Saint-Omer and commerce during the 19th Century

During the 19th Century the area around Saint-Omer was rich in industry. This area was commercial and good at it. Unlike many of the towns in the Nord Pas-de-Calais Saint-Omer was not a mining town but it did follow its commercial roots and was very wealthy as a result. Saint-Omer had a very broad base of commercial activities. There were sugar refineries, flour mills, breweries (otherwise known as *brasseries*), malteries, alcohol distilleries for industrial and pharmaceutical uses, gin distilleries, salt refineries, paper manufacturers, pottery makers, a pipe and tobacco industry, and vinegar distilleries and mustard manufacturers. In regard to the last two, two factories here produced 1 200 000 litres of vinegar, 280 000 kilos of *Moutarde Blanche* which is Dijon in style and an incredible 1 400 000 kilos of *Moutarde grise du Nord*, literally, Grey Mustard of the North. (24). Having researched extensively to try and find you tasting notes on what was once a very popular mustard indeed, the closest that I have been able to come up with is a possible example of the pot which unsurprisingly is not that dissimilar to the weighty pots used for grain mustard from Dijon.

Due to the numerous abattoirs that were located in the town there was also a sizeable leather goods industry here. Refined, high-quality lingerie was also produced here.

As is the case today there was a strong presence of manufacturers devoted to serving the construction industry. Cement was and still is produced at nearby Lumbres. Around fifteen million bricks were made annually as well as twenty three million tiles within a six mile radius of Saint-Omer. There are still in existence some small brick factories in the area (Ruminghem and Arques) that might well be able to produce bricks in the authentic old fashioned style useful for renovation. There were also ceramics and foundry firms, soap and hessian makers, bleach manufacturers and also those who produced the humble brush.

And still we haven't got to one of the biggest success stories of the area – ARC International. Most of us have probably eaten from a plate or bowl, and drunk wine or orange juice from a Paris goblet that was made in Arques. The company was created in 1825 and started its life as *La Verrerie Cristallerie D'Arques*. It has changed its name several times and for the time being is known to us all as ARC International . It was bought outright in 1926 by the Durand family who still have considerable interest in the company. Today it produces a variety of lines from 'cheap and cheerful' to 'Oh my God – put that down!'

Despite enormous international competition and large scale redundancies over recent years this ancient manufacturer battles on with considerable success. There is an excellent glassworks tour and factory shop which is well worth visiting.

Saint-Omer was connected to the railway network in 1848 (Stephenson's Rocket hit the rails in 1829) and became a major railway hub. It is much less importance today however railways buffs can see the Orient Express pass through the station on Thursday afternoons.

Two great visionaries of the town and 3rd Republican moderates were Louis Martel and Charles Jonnart. Both pushed for the development of the town believing that it would become a *Grand Ville* of great importance once again. Their energy and perseverance saw to it that the beautiful *Jardin Public* was constructed.

Memorial in the Jardin Public to Charles Jonnart 1857 – 1927 © Photo Jonathan Caton

The *Jardin Public* is magnificent at any time of the year with a wonderful variety of plants, trees and the most beautiful flower beds bursting with colour. It is in fact an Arboretum of some standing with superb examples of trees from Europe, America and Asia. The creative mind behind this wonderful 20 hectare piece of landscaped paradise was an engineer called François Ernest Guinoiseau who created the park between 1892 and 1898. Aside the Arboretum are beautifully designed flower beds known locally as the *Jardin à l'anglaise.* Dotted in amongst the winding paths and soaring trees are duck ponds, playgrounds as well as a small zoo. There is a classic bandstand popular for wedding day photographs and around this several times a year there are various *Gourmet* or *Pétanque* festivals.

Saint-Omer Rulers:	Third Republic up to 1940
	Fourth Republic 1946 – 1958
	Fifth Republic 1958 – present day
Throne of Great Britain	
& Northern Ireland:	Edward VII (b.1841) k.fr 1901 – 1910
	George V (b.1865) k.fr 1910 – 1936
	Edward VIII (b.1894) 1936 Abdicated
	George VI (b.1895) k.fr 1936 -1952
	Elizabeth II (b.1926) qu.fr 1952 –

KEY DATES

1909   Louis Blériot makes first flight from Les Baraques to Dover in 35 mins

1914   British Expeditionary Force (BEF) make Saint-Omer their GHQ

1914   Royal Flying Corps (RFC) makes Saint-Omer their GHQ

1914   Lord Roberts VC dies in Saint-Omer after a four day visit

1914   Sir John French made C-in-C of the BEF and stationed in Saint-Omer

1914   4th December King George and the Prince of Wales visit the RFC and Saint-Omer and are met by the French President Raymond Poincaré and Général Joffre

1915   Marechal Pétain visits Saint-Omer

1915   Prime Minster Asquith visits and holds talks with Général Joffre and M Millerand in Saint-Omer

1915   George V and Queen Mary visit RFC and BEF HQ. They stay in 20 rue St Bertin at the former Hôtel de Berghes – opposite No 37 – Sir John French's house

1917   July Queen Mary visits RFC and Saint-Omer

1918   On the 11th November at 11.00 o'clock the First World War comes to an end after an estimated combatant death toll of 8.5 million people

1940   German forces arrive in Saint-Omer starting a 1245 day occupation

1941   Douglas Bader treated in a Saint-Omer hospital for injuries sustained after baling out over the Pas-de-Calais

1941   At behest of German flying ace a replacement leg is dropped by RAF for Bader in 'Leg Operation.'

1944   Saint-Omer liberated by Polish troops on Tuesday 5th September 1944

1953   Queen Elizabeth II's coronation

1973   Douglas Bader invited to Saint-Omer to witness the presentation of the Légion d'Honneur to those who helped in his attempted escape

Headquarters to the British Expeditionary Force and the Spiritual home of the Royal Air Force 1914 – 1917

As we fast approach the centenary of the start of the First World War I am going to recount some interesting stories, events and characters all of whom I hope will make your visit to the town a little more meaningful. Geographically speaking Saint-Omer was for the majority of the First World War not much further than thirty miles from the fighting on the Western Front. The town maintained its access to the sea via Gravelines and had excellent links to the front by road, rail and for the first time; air. The town itself changed. Not only was it a town in which were billeted considerable numbers of the British Expeditionary Force, The Royal Flying Corps, Medical staff and journalists but between the 12th October 1914 and 1916 it was the Headquarters for the British Army. After 1916 the BEF HQ transferred to Montreuil-sur-Mer but a considerable number of British troops remained, staying at the *Caserne de Cygne*, which is now a car park between *Place Victor Hugo* and the *Grand Place*. As the Head Quarters the town had frequent visitors from Royalty, high rank or office but also maintained a core residence of military staff which was necessary to 'administer' the war. The town adapted and visitors to the town might have been easily fooled 'at street level' into thinking that they were in an English town. Black and white signs in English similar to those found in London and towns all over England were erected. Signs such as 'Motor cars and cycles prohibited' or 'Speed Limit: Cars 10 miles per hour, Lorries 6 miles per hour' were most common.

There was an abundance of British Goods in the shops and trade flourished. Smart English style light brown shoes for Officers 'en cuir jaune' (light brown leather) were on sale in the town as well as York Ham and best 'English whisky'. Tabacs were also well stocked to meet the demand for a most popular form of communication at the time – the postcard.

One local newspaper that is still in circulation today, 'L'Indépendant' gives us near daily accounts of progress at the front, news and opinion from London as well as events reported from an international point of view. The paper reports extensively on the curiosity that the British troops attracted. The local people of Saint-Omer as we know were well used to the presence of the military but it is interesting to learn how on Saturday 3rd April 1915 for example there was an article published entitled 'Les Anglais à Saint-Omer' describing the neatness and order of the sentries 'standing to' or 'at attention'. The report comments upon the meticulous appearance and attention to detail that the sentries gave in carrying out their duties. It goes on to give us a picture of how the town changed with its new traffic signs, afternoon tea and 'Barmaids'.

So it was on Monday 3rd August 1914 at 15h30 that war was declared against France by Germany. The substantial French military presence in the town aroused much patriotism and the French 8ème RI Dragoon Guards led by Colonel Doyen (killed on the 7th October 1914) departed for the front on the 5th at 8.00 o'clock to jubilant cries of "Vive La France, Vive l'Armée" and even "Vive La Guerre!". Within a year this same proud regiment had endured 3 213 deaths, lost 4 out of its 7 colonels, had been awarded eighty seven Légions d'Honneur and 582 other medals for bravery. A street in Saint-Omer was named to commemorate their bravery in 1927 called rue du 8ème de Ligne and below you see the memorial erected to the 8th Dragoon Guards in Place de Verdun. Departing also on the same day from Saint-Omer was the 27th Artillery Regiment led by Colonel Clement.

Memorial to the 8ème R.I. in Place de Verdun © Photo Jonathan Caton

Sunday 30th August 1914

Written just weeks after the start of hostilities the following poem was published on the front page of *L'Indépendant*. This was an era when poetry was often used to voice opinion as well as stimulate thought. This particular poem was written by an unknown

Belgian Officer stationed at the front. It might not be of particular literary merit but it does conjure up the defiant spirit of the French and her allies in facing up to the German adversary. The poem reads as follows:

Aux Soldats du Kaiser – To the Kaisers' Soldiers

Tristes mangeurs de choucroûte / You sad sauerkraut eaters

Qui rêviez de Paris / Who dreamt of Paris

Librement prendre la route / Be on your way

Vite les Belges vous ont dit / The Belgians quickly told you

Halte! on ne pause pas / Halt! You can't stop here

Car jamais votre engeance / Since your mob

En Gaule n'entrera! / Will never enter Gaul

Sentinelles de la France / Sentries of France

De vos hordes sauvages / Will break the spirit of your

Nous briserons l'élan / Hordes of surging savages

Les Belges avec courage / The courageous Belgians

Ont bravé le Uhlan* / Braved the Uhlan*

*= The Uhlan were German regiments of Light Cavalry armed with lances, sabres and pistols

As a consequence of the BEF and RFC using the town as their respective GHQ's the population of Saint-Omer mushroomed. Schools and *Lycées* were requisitioned, military hospitals were established, tents pitched up in cobbled and gracious courtyards. The canal, *Quai du Commerce*, the station and *'routes nationales'* leading in and out of the town were all heavily congested with traffic. Reinforcements, munitions, materials and supplies rumbled through the town. Even a prisoner of war camp was set up at a nearby commune of Saint-Omer: Saint Martin-au-Laërt. Officers were billeted in some of the larger houses in the town. The Royal Flying Corps commanders were accommodated in a large 19th Century red brick stucco building called Chateau Lansel ou *Château des Bruyères* owned by the Deschamps de Pas family and located in the commune of Longuenesse to which the owners were invited to a rather boisterous dinner party as way of thanks! (25)

RFC HQ Château des Bruyères, Longuenesse © Stéphane Milamon

A 'GHQ' has to find premises for many functions and large swathes of the town centre were 'leased' to the army during its occupancy, notably houses in *rue de Dunkerque, rue Faidherbe, rue Carnot, La Grande Place, Place Victor Hugo, rue Henri-Dupuis, rue Allent* and *Saint Bertin*.

The British Army's HQ in Saint-Omer - 37 rue Saint-Bertin. Opposite this house George V stayed when he visited Saint-Omer in 1915. This picture is by Adrian Hill, War Artist

© Imperial War Museum, London

For the majority of soldiers, airmen and medics this would have been their first taste of the Continent. One officer commented that he liked Saint-Omer very much because it reminded him of the wide streets of Kensington. However soon after the arrival of the British forces a 'liquor law' had to be drawn up banning the consumption of alcohol except during strictly regulated times and the consumption of absinthe or the Green Fairy (*La Fée Verte*) was banned altogether. However on the whole the townsfolk rubbed along very nicely with their new residents. One popular haunt for the troops and in particular for Officers was the Café de L'Harmonie owned by a Monsieur E Vincent situated at *10 Grand Place* and history relates, unsurprisingly, that there was the allure of a pretty auburn haired waitress called Jeanne. This café is now a soft furnishing store called Lionet Décor.

The Hôtel de Ville and Saturday Market by war artist Adrian Hill around 1915

© Imperial War Museum, London

British soldiers parading on Place Foch c1915
© Société Académique des Antiquaires de la Morinie

The *Grand Place* was a natural Parade ground for the BEF as well as being the social hub of the town. As is found today, cafés, restaurants and shops were dotted around the square and the Theatre in the *Hôtel de Ville* regularly put on shows. Our friend Smith Pearse tells us that he was amused by a poster situated in *rue de Calais* that requested that theatre goers kindly arrived on time for performances, the English translation to these people was addressed to "The Comings Tardily!"

There is also a lot of evidence for the bi-partisanship between the French and the British. For example on Wednesday 28th October 1915 there is advertised a 'Match de Foot-ball' between 'l'Union Sportive de Saint-Omer vs Télégraphistes Anglais' – The final score is not recorded. Another example is a concert that took place on Sunday 19th March 1916. The sixty orchestral players were made up of both nationalities and the programme of pieces reflected this:

160

Beethoven: 1ˢᵗ Symphony

Saint-Saëns: Prélude du Déluge

Lebane: Souvenir de Mar del Plata

Hasselmanns: Patrouille (Harp Solo)

Léo Delibes: Ballet de Coppélia

E MacDowell: Thy Beaming Eyes

Schumann: The Three Grenadiers

Berlioz: Marche de la Damnation de Faust

God Save the King and La Marseillaise

All the proceeds went to the Red Cross. The concert was received well and a good review followed later that week. British Military music was much admired and well attended concerts were given regularly in the Grand Place.

This *Entente Cordiale* spirit is taken up by the Hon J W Fortescue in his book *The British Soldiers Guide to Northern France and Flanders* published by *The Times*. In it he writes that the French Low Countries and Northern France were the oldest and most familiar of the British Army's campaigning grounds. Up until the First World War there were five key groups of campaigns (not including the 100 Years War): William III (1691 – 1697), Marlborough 1702 – 1711, Stair, Wade, Cumberland and Ligonier 1742 – 1748, Duke of York 1793 – 1794 and Wellington 1815. He concludes that 'In all these cases France was the enemy but with World War One that gallant nation became our friend.'

The French curiosity with the British way of life continued to be publicised in the local press. On Wednesday 12ᵗʰ January 1916 an article goes into some detail about the ritual surrounding a Scottish Regiment's ceremony for New Year. The celebration takes place on New Year's Eve and requires the services of the oldest and youngest soldiers in the regiment.

The oldest dons a white beard and presents himself at the entrance to the barracks. Upon doing so he demands to speak to the Sentry of the watch. He is then led to the assembled regiment where upon he is given a glass of wine or whisky. There he stands until the clock strikes midnight where upon he is asked to leave without delay. This done, the youngest of the regiment arrives but his way is barred by the extended bayonet of the sentry who barks: 'Halt! Who goes there?'

'It's the New Year!' cries the young soldier. The way is opened for him and he is hoisted up and taken into the middle of his brave comrades '*Entre et prends place au milieu de ses braves*'. Where upon the bagpipes are inflated and 'New Year' is paraded around the barracks in triumph to the accompaniment of Scottish Airs.

The British soldiers were very popular here and left good impressions. An article printed on Tuesday 16th February 1915 for the same newspaper entitled '*Les Soldats Anglais dans le Nord*' tells us that the French '*on les adore parce que les soldats anglais sont généreux. Bien payé. Ils payent bien*'. In other words they adore the British Soldiers because they are generous. They are paid well and they pay well.

Field Marshal Roberts VC

Due to the elevated status that the town now received it was no stranger to visiting dignitaries, French or English, Military or State. One such person was Field Marshal Roberts VC. He arrived in France around the weekend of the 14th / 15th November 1914. He had turned down an invitation to attend a conference at Caxton Hall that weekend because of his military commitments in Saint-Omer: an inspection of the Indian Troops. This was reported in *L'Indépendant* of Monday 16th November 1914. The following Wednesday the headlines were very different and covered large amounts of news space in most newspapers right across Europe. They were all reporting the sudden death on Saturday 14th November 1914 of Field Marshal Roberts from a chest infection (pneumonia to be precise) whilst residing at *52 rue Carnot*. He was 82 years old. His body was taken with great ceremony to the *Hôtel de Ville* where it stayed in the vestibule which had been specially consecrated for the occasion as he was naturally Church of England, whilst awaiting transportation to England for a State Funeral. As we can see from the photo below the procession was something very special. Roberts's body was mounted onto a gun carriage, draped with the Union flag and pulled by six magnificent horses. Soldiers from the 2nd Battalion Royal Irish, the 6th Battalion Gordon Highlanders, The Warwickshire Royal Horse Artillery and the 36th Brigade of the Royal Field artillery provided the escort. As the body reached *Place Foch* the soldiers bowed their heads and onlookers removed their hats. Clergy stood at the front of the *Hôtel de Ville* in their long white robes waiting to receive the body. To the left facing the *Hôtel de Ville* a file of dignitaries is waiting to pay their respects. The central flagpole of the *Hôtel* is displaying the Union Jack at half-mast.

52 rue Carnot. The house where Lord Roberts died © Photo Jonathan Caton

Lord Roberts's body being conveyed to the Hôtel de Ville, Saint-Omer

© Société Académique des Antiquaires de la Morinie

The following day *L'Indépendant* gives over a whole page to the coverage of Lord Roberts' body returning to London and his proposed internment in St Paul's Cathedral where he rests today. Today many visitors to the town enquire who Lord Roberts was especially as the house where he died on *rue Carnot* has the rare privilege in France of being adorned with a Blue Plaque.

A rare honour. The blue plaque commemorating the house in which Lord Roberts died,
52 rue Carnot, Saint-Omer © Photo Jonathan Caton

So in response to the curious amongst us here is his life story in brief.

Frederick Sleigh Roberts was born in Cawnpore in India in 1832. He joined the Royal Artillery in 1851 and throughout his long and distinguished military career he took part in the Umbeyla Campaign (1863), Abyssinian Campaign (1867-1868), the Lushai Campaign (1871-1872), the Second Afghan War, the Battle of Kandahar (1880) the

Second Boer War (1899-1902) and finally acted as a Field Marshal for the first months of World War 1.

He took a prominent role in the quashing of the Indian Uprising of 1857-58. This series of disturbances led to India coming under direct rule of the British Crown and no longer from the East India Company – it also sowed the seeds for the final overthrow of British rule and the rise of Indian Independence which came about in 1947. Due to the military success in suppressing the Indian Uprisings Roberts was awarded the Victoria Cross in 1858. Aside his VC he was made a Knight of the Order of the Garter, Knight Grand Cross of the Order of the Bath, Order of Merit, Knight Grand Cross of the Order of the Star of India and finally a Knight Grand Cross of the Order of the Indian Empire. Two notable posts that he held were that of Commander-in-Chief in India (1885-1893) and also Supreme Commander in South Africa during the Boer War. He was made an Earl in 1901 and apart from being referred to as 'Bobs' as a nickname by his men, his official title was Lord Roberts, 1st Earl of Kabul and Kandahar. His body was taken from Saint-Omer to London to lie in state at Westminster Hall before receiving a State Funeral and burial in the Crypt of St Paul's Cathedral, London.

Frederick Sleigh Roberts, 1ˢᵗ Earl Roberts by John Singer Sargent, oil on canvas, 1906

© *National Portrait Gallery, London*

Back in 1914 the local paper *L'Indépendant* covered far more than local news. Founded in 1849 it was a broadsheet in dimension and covered international news as well as listing those getting married next Saturday for instance. As the rising cost in human life became daily news, local papers such as this publication started including in each edition from October 1914 a list of the local French dead and what was referred to as the *Champ d'Honneur* or The Field of Honour. Two more columns were added shortly afterwards listing French Prisoners of War and, in November, the French Missing lists. Periodically *L'Indépendant* would publicize British figures given out from London by Prime Minister Lord Asquith. An example being on Wednesday 18th November 1914 when Asquith announced to the House of Commons that up until the end of October 1914 the British mortality rate was approximately 57 000 men. Therefore in approximately 89 days of war the British were being killed at a rate of 640 men a day (26). Bear in mind this is a few months before the utter carnage at the Battle of the Somme.

L'Indépendant also reported on 'Life in the Trenches' making their articles more interesting by examining the subject from the perspective of other nationalities. For example in the edition of 27th March 1916 the focus was on '*Les Tranchées Anglaises*' another week it could equally be French, Belgium, Irish, Australian or Canadian trenches under the spotlight. Curiously enough frivolous British news squeezed in; for example in the same edition there is an article reporting on an apparent lack of cigarettes at Newnham College, Cambridge "Cigarettes Please – Student girls demonstrate for not being able to smoke for a lack of fags."

The differences between cultures has always fascinated the French and hence an article that was written for the 25th April 1915 edition focuses on the importance of being able to speak at least one other language and it recounts the following story:

De l'Utilité de Parler les langues – The usefulness of speaking languages

The story tells of two Generals, one French, one English who met to discuss a forthcoming joint attack against the Germans. The English General opened up the conversation in French. Unfortunately it transpired that the French General did not understand one word of what his counterpart was saying. And he said so. On hearing the French General's unintelligible French to his English ear, the general thought he detected something of an Alsatian accent. '*Spreken sie deutsch?*' he enquired. '*Jah vol*' came back the reply and so the forthcoming attack was discussed in German.

British newspapers and magazines also covered events that were occurring in Saint-Omer. For instance an article appeared in *The Sphere* magazine on June 12th 1915 reporting a visit to the town and area by the British Prime Minister Asquith.

Mr Asquith at the front – How his five days were spent.

"The PM's visit to France which lasted from Sunday 30th May to Thursday 3rd June has naturally aroused a great deal of interest. "On the day following his arrival at Headquarters, immediately after breakfast," writes Mr Percival Landon in The Daily Telegraph; Mr Asquith motored to a height some distance from Cassel. As he arrived the burning town of Ypres, which has been bombarded on most days during the last fortnight, was caught by the north-east wind, and a heavier volume of drifting brown smoke rose from the unhappy place.

"Mr Asquith paid unusual attention to the scene of the fighting on 'Hill 60' in April and to the wrecked town of Mesines, which after a shelling was left uninhabitable and wrested from us on November 1st."

"From this neighbourhood the PM went on to luncheon with the General commanding an army corps, and took the opportunity of saying a few words of praise to a brigade which had that day been relieved after a long spell of incessant fighting in the trenches."

"After an inspection of a hospital Mr Asquith amused himself with a visit to a factory near the front which has been turned into a washing station for troops returned from the trenches.

A visit to the Royal Flying Corps began Mr Asquith's next day. He was shown over the ground by the commander, and witnessed the ascent of two biplanes.

The PM then motored to luncheon with the commander of the First Army and spent the afternoon in visiting various centres. Among the first were the Indian troops under Sir James Willcocks. There was a display here which had no rival throughout Mr Asquith's stay in the country. Khaki shears away much of the panoply of Indian life, and those who went expecting to see the glories of the Madra or 19th Cavalry regiments, or the Imperial Cadet Corps, found in the businesslike outfit of all, the keenness of the infantry, and the extraordinarily sound condition of the horses more than compensation for the loss of silver lace or leopard-skin saddle-cloths. Two brigades, consisting chiefly of Sikhs, Gurkhas, and Dogras, lined the roads as the PM drove by.

"Mr Asquith had now completed his chief work of inspection. He spent a comparatively quiet day. In the morning of June 2nd he visited several of the departments of headquarters, and in the afternoon he received General Joffre, who was accompanied by General Foch and Mr Millerand, the French Minister of War, with whom he had a conference for half an hour. Later in the day he motored to Dunkirk and Bergues. On Thursday the PM contented himself with a few private visits to headquarter departments and after luncheon took his leave of the Commander-in-Chief, leaving for England about three o'clock".

170

Saint-Omer's Hospitals during World War 1

Saint-Omer had a great many hospitals before the start of the First World War and the number grew as the volume of wounded from the frontline rapidly increased. The town played host to the 7th and 58th (Scottish) General Hospitals, the 59th (Northern) General Hospital as well as the 4th, 7th, 9th and 10th Canadian and New Zealand Stationary hospitals and finally 1st, 2nd, 17th and 18th Australian Clearing Stations. A British Army hospital was also created in Longuenesse at La Malassise - now a prestigious college and lycée. The difference between the General Hospitals and Stationary Hospitals in the First World War were that the 'Generals' had beds for up to a 1000 patients whilst the Stationary Hospital offered the same level of care but on a smaller scale with a capacity of up to 500 beds.

It is interesting to learn how these hospitals were created and in order to illustrate this I would like to turn your attention to the British 59th Territorial Northern General Hospital. This hospital stemmed from the Territorial Army Hospitals created in 1908. They were not a volunteer outfit. There were originally fifty of these hospitals situated in various parts of England. They were intended to be able to treat 504 people in beds but by 1916 this had risen to 2166. As a result of the appalling slaughter of the Battle of the Somme it was decided that the Territorial Force Hospitals should create seven more Hospitals to help cope with the deluge of horrifically wounded and traumatised men. The 59th was formed in Blackpool in April 1917. It was then transferred to Amiens in which is approximately 110 kms due south of Saint-Omer in May 1917. It remained in Amiens until the 14th July 1917 when it transferred to *l'Hôpital Militaire* which was once the premises of the English Jesuit College in rue Saint-Bertin. The hospital remained in Saint-Omer until 26th May 1918 when it transferred to Rouen until it was disbanded the following May. God only knows how many people were treated during its stay in Saint-Omer but we know that it was hit during an air raid on 1st October 1917 resulting in damage and casualties. One often overlooks the immense part that horses played during this conflict. There was a also a Veterinary Hospital in the *'Quartier Esquerdes'*.

From the thousands of troops, airmen, military personnel, medical staff and local people that were billeted or lived here I would like to present some at complete random. Thanks to the care taken by many of the relatives of those who took part in the conflict and who kept dairies I was lucky enough to read their accounts in the Reading Room at the Imperial War Museum where they are available to consult.

Dorothy Field VAD Nurse

The first person concerns a nurse called Dorothy Field. She was a VAD nurse (VAD being Voluntary Aid Detachment) for a time at 10th Stationary Hospital in Saint-Omer, located in rue Edouard Devaux. The professional and voluntary nurses (VAD) and FANY's (First Aid Nursing Yeomanry) were held in enormous esteem. The horrors that they were exposed to day in, day out were relentless and gruesome and much of it beyond our comprehension. The following poem was written by a soldier simply identified as 'O'Rourke' and serving in the Cameron Highlanders on 9th September 1916. His verse sums up the feelings that the soldiers had for these brave, courageous and highly necessary individuals:

You have heard the deeds of soldiers and of sailors at sea

But I am sure that on this point you will with me agree

That the sisters in the hospital wards who nurse us back to health

Are precious far more precious than the winning power of wealth

See the smile upon their face as they pass by to and fro

It helps you bear your burden with that smile they always show

You may be suffering lots of pain and feeling very dread

But now that pain is soothed and eased when she comes round to your bed

They converse with you freely what every soldier loves

It is the touch of nature and not the touch of gloves

They give you every comfort that is possible to be had

Let you be a College youth or just a working lad

It's a God send that in England we have ladies such as these

Who will always do the best they can their study is to please.

Nurse Field mentions in a postcard written on January 16th 1916 to a friend that there was a postal allowance for the BEF and RFC personnel of two letters and four cards a month which was not enough to keep in touch. She adds though that she is in with a mix of nationalities comprising English, French, Belgians and Russians "all spending time pretending to learn each others' languages".

Nurse Field has a collection of small pocket sized dairies of the time called 'The Soldier's Own Diary'. Apart from the monthly calendar, there is a whole range of curious and interesting information stuffed in between the days of the twelve months for example 'How to navigate by use of the nocturnal sky' or 'Finding your way by the positioning of the daytime Sun' or 'How to cut a glass bottle safely', 'how to make a soap shaker which is ideal for using up odd ends of soap but is also very useful for the washing up bowel'. Another explains how to extract natural sea salt from sea water using a tin, wind and a piece of cloth!

There was huge pride being a volunteer nurse and this came not only from the volunteer but from the organizations themselves. We see an example of this in the official communications from the Red Cross to Miss Field on April 16th 1915. They write:

"Here is the Red Cross identity disc which you may like to wear to remind you that you belong to our Society. (The British Red Cross Society) You are the first representatives of the British Red Cross VAD Members who have been actually handed over to the War Office under new terms of service. I hope that you will be happy in your work and that you will do your very best to make a good name for the VAD members that follow you. … Please write and tell me if you ever have the time what work you are doing and how you enjoy it, and if there is anything that I can do for you here at home, let me know."

VAD nurses like many of the other volunteer services and organizations had to conform to the many Kings 'Rules and Regs'. For instance, we know that when Nurses had been out on the town to official functions they had to 'trot' to positions. One such notice appears on the back of a programme for a theatrical evening:

After the entertainment has finished it reads "Sisters will fall in by Hospitals at a smart trot ... and will be marched ... by the nearest route to their quarters.

The notice continues
"No COMPLIMENTS will be paid to officers after dark."
By order
D Hard.Luck
General

I doubt whether this was the General's name but it certainly is in keeping with the forbidding nature of the regulations.

Miss Dorothy Field survived the horrors of World War 1 and went on to use her valuable experience in Saint-Omer and other field Hospitals in France when she volunteered as a VAD nurse for the next global conflict World War Two – 21 years later.

Lance Corporal F GOWER Bus Driver AOCA No: 082418 1915 – 1920

Lance Corporal Gower enlisted on Tuesday 4th May 1915 in Hastings. He was attached to the Mechanical Transport Army Service Corps. He was sent to Devizes 248 Company which formed part of the 20th Division Ammunition Column. The Company left Devizes on Monday 19th July 1915 with 100 lorries and 4 mobile workshops. They drove to Avonmouth for departure. They crossed the Channel by night and arrived in Rouen on Thursday 22nd July 1915.

Gower with the Company left Rouen on Sunday 25th July. It took four days to reach Vieux-Berquin (near Hazebrouck). Here they were told that their column of lorries was too great for the size of their destination so half would have to report to GHQ Saint-Omer – Lance Corporal Gower was amongst the latter.

In his reminiscences he tells up that in the first week of September 1915 he noticed more London Buses arriving in Saint-Omer, many of them being driven by drivers who had come to France at the start of the conflict and who could now under the terms of their original contracts 'take their tickets' as dictated by the rules for the "reserve" formation. I am speculating in saying this meant that they could 'demob' and go home.

As a consequence there was a recruitment drive in Saint-Omer for experienced bus drivers. Gower who had driven double deckers in Hastings of the type used in London volunteered. His application was successful and so he started driving a London Bus in Saint-Omer. A new Bus Company was formed in the town called the 16th Auxiliary Bus Company. The company comprised of 75 Double Deckers and 25 American Locomobile Char-à-Bancs plus one or two workshops. These were divided into four sections.

All the buses had a circular logo on each side showing a circle which symbolized a "one penny" piece and around it were the words "all the way". Each bus was manned by two drivers. The main function of Gower's job was to transport troops from one place to another either "Up the Line" or "Down the line".

"A Penny All The Way": London Motor Buses on the Amiens Road 1918 by Adrian Hill

© *Imperial War Museum, London*

Sometimes he was sent to Calais to meet a boat. When there was heavy fighting two buses were detailed to each of the Casualty Clearing Stations in the area taking the walking wounded back to hospitals down the line. There was very little time for relaxation as for the most part they were working around the clock. If free time were given much of it was spent "doing repairs and cleaning".

In January 1917 GHQ moved camps and the 16th Auxiliary Bus Company was broken up and sections were sent to different locations along the western front. LC Gower's was to the 5th Army HQ stationed at Beauval. He tells us that due to driving frequently on rough terrain the bodywork of the buses deteriorated despite a high level of maintenance and care and not long after the Big Push began on the 8th August 1918 he was sent to Rouen for repairs (4th Heavy Repair Unit). Here they replaced the old coachwork with a lorry body. This alteration removed half of their load capacity and so their maximum passenger number was limited considerably.

Gower survived the war and after the Armistice was signed on Monday 11th November 1918 he was sent to nearby Wissant on Tuesday 23rd December 1919 where there was the vehicle reception park. He was finally demobbed on Tuesday 13th April 1920 after 5 years service in Mechanical transport, Army Service Corps.

The British Army requisitioned 300 London 'B type' buses at the start of the conflict because of the acute lack of transport at the time. As we learn from Lance Corporal Gower's account they stayed in service throughout the war. After the armistice they were re-enrolled into their more traditional routes in London – usually routes 8 and 9. A total of 900 such buses were used in France and Belgium in a whole variety of roles from ambulances, mobile communication units through the mediums of the wireless and even as pigeon lofts.

They were affectionately given the name of 'Old Bill' after the wartime cartoon character created by Bruce Bairnsfather. There is an original example of an 'Old Bill' permanently displayed in the Imperial War Museum in London and at the Museum of Transport, Covent Garden, London, to both of whom I express my thanks for their help in my research.

Rifleman R E HARRIS 3rd Battalion New Zealand Rifle Brigade

Rifleman Harris has left us some very illuminating accounts in his diaries from his brief stay in Saint-Omer. He records that on Wednesday 12th July 1916 whilst in the trenches he discovers that he has measles "out thick". Next day on the 13th July "along with six others he is ousted out of the trenches and after three ambulance journeys via Bailleul he arrives at Saint-Omer" … "Bailleul where we had some lunch and go on to Saint-Omer in the afternoon. This is a large Hospital of Marquees. It is an English hospital and the food is very small in quantity and of poor quality for a hospital, in fact we get so little that it is not sufficient to keep ourselves warm. We have more and better food in the trenches. I have no temperature and do not feel sick, all of us have a slight cold, the measles being of the mildest form. We spend seven days here. Each place we stopped at we had to give name and number so from the time we got into Hospital, these particulars were taken no less than six times.

On the Thursday 20th July 1916 Harris writes that 'a bunch of us leave the hospital after dinner and march into Saint-Omer where we spend the night. There are three German Prisoners in the top of the same building.' We enter a church [Cathedral], because in this country the churches are all very beautiful inside. The English churches being very plain compared to them. A small party of us is shown round by a priest. Amongst other things we are shown the tomb of an Irish Saint (Saint Erkembode). The priest asks if there are any Irishmen amongst us, there is one, to whom he gives a picture of the tomb and tells him if he carries it with him it will protect him from rheumatism. The priest spoke in a mixture of English and French and we were not able to understand all he said even if his English, like our French was not always correctly pronounced, he was probably largely book taught'.

Harris left Saint-Omer the next day and rejoined his fellow soldiers in their trench by 10.00 am on Saturday 22nd July.

On Friday 15th September 1916 Harris was near fatally wounded when a bullet passed through his chest 'all I felt was a warm sting which I hardly felt at all'. It soon was apparent to him that the entry hole was tiny and the real damage was in fact a gaping hole in his back. He writes almost nonchalantly concerning his rescue by some 'Tommies' belonging to the West Lancashire Regiment. They stretchered his battered body from where he was found slumped in the trenches back to the safety of a field hospital behind the lines. He writes "They passed a battery that was not in operation at the time. One of them rushed over with a bottle of brandy and offered it. I thought it was very good of him but not wanting any myself I thanked him and asked him to let the chaps who were carrying me have a nip as they were rather exhausted, having been working all day with no rest. He offered them the bottle and they did not need to be asked twice'.

With horrific wounds Harris was shipped back to 'Blighty' on Saturday 23rd September 1916.

2nd Lt Richard LINTOTT 2/5th City of London Battalion No 11 Platoon London Rifle Brigade

Lt Richard Lintott was trained for the first part of the war very close to Saint-Omer in Blendecques at the Cadet Training School. His diary dates from early on in the war and in it he notes the death of Lord Roberts in Saint-Omer. He writes:

"November 16th 1914 Breakfast 6.00am. Cleared up room and moved off at 8.15am. Marched 26km to Hazebrouck had lunch at 11.15am, soon after it began to rain and continued until 2.00pm. Got very wet, arrived Hazebrouck 3.00pm. Heard of Lord Roberts's death at Saint-Omer this morning. Very sorry to leave after comfortable billet at the convent. Billeted in a Club at Hazebrouck 55 men in the billiard room."

There are many accounts of the Christmas Day truce of 1914 and Lintott has given us a detailed account of what he was up to on this memorable day. He recounts:

Friday December 25th Christmas Day 1914

"At 6.00am we moved to the 2nd line of [defence] with all our goods and chattels and then had breakfast, no fatigues today at all. At 1.00pm had dinner [of] stewed rabbit (Lintott was an accomplished hunter) Christmas Pudding and Rum. After dinner we walked up to the firing line and there we found all our fellows out of the trenches talking to the Germans who had come out of theirs also. They were burying some dead who had been lying out since October 21st. We all (German and English) stood bareheaded round the grave while a German Officer read the service. We exchanged cigarettes etc and one

179

gave me a clip of cartridges. Then we returned and had tea. Rations were drawn at 5.30pm and with them a present for each man from Princess Mary, a card from the King and Queen and one from the 4th Division. At 10.00pm just as we were about to start for the firing line I slipped and fell off the bridge into the 6ft trench through the ice and got wet through to the skin so I had to return to Ploegsteert. I arrived at the 'Au Charron' at 1.00pm. [Quarters] let me in and gave me a dry shirt, socks and had a good rub down and some rum and wrapped myself up well and went to sleep. This ended a Christmas Day which I shall never forget in all my life".

It was his last Christmas in his short life. 'Lt Lintott was killed at Fortuin on Monday 3rd May 1915 by one of our own shells, whilst asleep in one of our reserve trenches, after four days' action in the second battle of Ypres.'

For his sister Nancy it was particularly poignant as his death coincided with her 21st Birthday. His body was never found and his name is carved on the Menin Gate at Ypres – (one of Saint-Omer's twin towns) along with 55,000 others of whom nobody was ever found.

Although we'll look in more detail at the Commonwealth War Graves Commission (CWGC) 'Souvenir' Cemetery at Longuenesse (a commune next to Saint-Omer) a little later on it is however appropriate to mention at this point the brave actions of two soldiers buried here, one of whom paid the ultimate price with his life and that is Corporal Frederick Noble.

In Plot I, Row A, Grave 57 you will find the grave of Cecil Reginald Noble who was a Corporal in the 2nd battalion of the Rifle Brigade (Prince Consort's Own). The Battalion was attempting to advance at Neuve Chapelle on Friday 12th March 1915 when it was stopped by heavy enemy machine gun fire and yards and yards of barbed wire, the story is now taken up by an actual account of what happened next.

It reads as follows:

"The wire had to be cut and instead of picking a number of men for the "suicidal task", No. 9665 CSM Harry Daniels asked his friend, No. 3697 A/Cpl Reginald "Tom" Noble to accompany him as he had on many dangerous night patrols in the past. The two friends, now armed with wire cutters, shook hands before setting out. They managed to cover the few yards to the wire unhurt and, lying on their backs, began to cut the lower strands. This done they raised themselves to sever the higher strands and finally to a kneeling position to reach the highest wires. It was then that Daniels was hit in the left thigh and dropped to the ground, after a few minutes he heard Noble gasp. Daniels asked, "What's up Tom" to which Noble replied, "I am hit in the chest, old man. Daniels managed to roll into a shell hole and apply rudimentary first aid to his wound, he remained there for four hours before trying to return to the battalion's trenches after dark when he was seen and picked up by his comrades. The attack meanwhile had been stopped. The VC citations for both men were identical. Corporal Noble died on the following day, 13 March 1915, aged 23 at a Clearing Station Hospital located in Longuenesse."

Recounted by kind permission of Andy Pay from his Private Collection of letters – The Pennefeather Letter. Harry Daniels went on to rise through the ranks to become Lieutenant H Daniels VC, MC.

A visit to Saint-Omer would not be complete without a visit to the historic aerodrome on the *Plateau des Bruyères*. Once home to twenty thousand soldiers of Napoléon's Army of England this plateau is in a sense the birthplace of the Royal Air Force as it was here that the Royal Flying Corps established their first home. It was for the duration of the First World War the biggest and most important airfield on the Western Front.

The British Services Memorial at Saint-Omer Aerodrome 'Per Ardua Ad Astra':
'Through Adversity to the Stars' © Photo Jonathan Caton

Used regularly today as the Saint-Omer Flying Club, this historic piece of turf was during the 1900's a showground to vast crowds. In the region of eight thousand spectators gathered here for the aviation spectacles, meanwhile it was in regular use by *'La Poste'* aviation service.

SOUVENIR DE L'AVIATION DE SAINT-OMER
Aérodrome du Plateau des Bruyères
Les Aviateurs Thomas, Jullerot, Mollien et Ernest Paul en plein vol

The early pioneers thrilling the crowds in the sky's above Saint-Omer. It is unlikely that there were ever more than two aeroplanes in flight at any given time, all the same this postcard expresses the huge enthusiasm for aeroplanes. © Stéphane Milamon

Unlike its past, the aerodrome today is relatively quiet and uncommercial, aside a popular restaurant that operates onsite near the immaculately kept British Services Memorial. It was only as recently as 2004 that this Memorial was erected to commemorate the five thousand Royal Flying Corps Personnel that once lived and worked here servicing or flying the aeroplanes of the fifty squadrons that passed through Saint-Omer at one time or another during the First World War. It is worth noting that the hanger that you see there today is the very same one that the Germans erected during World War Two and is now used by the St Omer flying club as well as making a wonderful venue for the occasional concert!

However the lack of commercial development makes it easy to imagine the drone of those early BE2A, SE5's, Nieurlet's and Sopwith Camels approaching the landing strip in an early crisp evening mist after a demanding sortie. Accompanied by the spluttering engines of the support vehicles at the ready to rush out over the bumpy ground to assist injured pilots and damaged aircraft.

One of the early senior officers of the Royal Flying Corps, Sir Frederick Sykes is recorded as saying at their arrival at Saint-Omer (Longuenesse) as:

"Morale within the RFC rose once the retreat ended (Reference to the 'Race to the Sea'), and gradually British Forces were able to move northward. RFC Headquarters moved from Fère-en-Tardenois to Abbeville (100kms south-west of Saint-Omer), where they stayed from 8th – 12th October, and then to Saint-Omer. The RFC had finally found a home – it would remain at Saint-Omer for the next two years. The staff receiving mail and settling into a daily routine that involved more than moving. Sykes's office and headquarters were in a red and white brick Chateau located on a hill between the town and aerodrome." (27)

The initial role of the RFC was to provide reconnaissance information for the army. As the conflict continued the role of the aeroplane became more combative and of vital importance to the successful outcome of military objectives. In the extract recorded below we read of the growing importance of the RFC to the success of the army on the ground as reported in The London Gazette from 10th July 1915.

"I have once more to call your Lordship's attention to the part taken by the Royal Flying Corps in the general progress of the campaign, and I wish particularly to mention the invaluable assistance they rendered in the operations described in this report, under the able direction of Major-General Sir David Henderson. The Royal Flying Corps in becoming more and more an indispensable factor in combined operations. In co-operation with the artillery, in particular, there has been continuous improvement both in the methods and the technical material employed. The ingenuity and technical skill displayed by the officers of the RFC, in effecting this improvement have been most marked.

Since my last despatch there has been a considerable increase both in the number and in the activity of German aeroplanes in our front. During this period there have been more than sixty combats in the air, in which not one British aeroplane has been lost. And these fights take place almost invariably over or behind German lines, only one hostile aeroplane has been brought down in our territory. Five more, however, have been definitely wrecked behind their own lines, and many have been chased down and forced to land in most unsuitable ground."

J.D.P. French, Field-Marshal, Commander-in-Chief, BEF

As the war continued and its huge material demands grew the role of the aerodrome changed. Saint-Omer was not a frontline airfield despite its close proximity to the fighting. This made it an ideal place along with the aerodrome at Candas (in Picardy approximately 120 kms south of Saint-Omer) to become one enormous recycling aircraft plant in addition to being an operational airfield. In the words of one commander Saint-Omer was a "gigantic factory and emporium". Their official names after December 1915 were No 1 Aircraft Depot (Saint-Omer) and No 2 AD (Candas).

At its peak during the third Battle of Ypres Salient in 1917 the RFC mechanics in Saint-Omer and Candas 'issued' 930 aircraft (sending aircraft from store to squadrons), 'reconstructed' 116 (repaired aircraft so that they could be issued) and 'erected' 113 (assembled aircraft that had been dismantled for transportation purposes for example)'. The contribution from these two outfits cannot be underestimated.

The Germans were also fully aware of the strategic and operational importance of Saint-Omer and as a result the town and aerodrome experienced more frequent and heavier air raids as the war went on in particular between 1917 and 1918. The air raids were responsible for many military and civilian deaths.

Despite the rapid improvement in engineering reliability there was still a weighty amount of pressure resting on the pilots and their ground crews. Navigation was also a major headache and precise map reading was essential. One episode concerning the dangers that can arise from inaccurate map reading appeared in *L'Indépendant* on Friday 30th June 1916. We learn that Lord Montagu announced to the House of Lords that recently an aeroplane of 'advanced capabilities' was flown from Farnborough by a Lt Littlewood accompanied by his Observer, Lt Grant.

They flew over the Channel, across the Pas-de-Calais, over Flanders and into occupied territory briefly touching down at Lille Aerodrome. It was not only the Germans who got a shock as I am sure did Lt's Grant and Littlewood. It was later disclosed that neither had flown in France and, as the journalist reports, nor had they a notion of the geography of France!

By March 1918 there were over 4300 technical personnel stationed in and around Saint-Omer – many of them working and living in temporary bessonneau canvas hangers and row upon row of Nissen huts as well as in the town. Permanent structures were considered and in 1917 a limited number of workshops and sheds were constructed.

Over fifty Squadrons stayed at one time or another in Saint-Omer but there are a few that have had and some still retain a special relationship with the town.

© Crown Copyright

9 Squadron – Motto: Per Noctum Volamus: Through the Night we fly

9 Squadron was formed in Saint-Omer in December 1914 from the HQ Wireless Telegraphy Unit under the Command of Captain Hugh Dowding. It was disbanded in 1915 and absorbed into other squadrons in the same year. From Saint-Omer the squadron flew BE2, Longhorn and Bleriot aircraft. 9 as an RAF Squadron went on to take part in operations to sink the Tirpitz pocket battleship on 12th November 1944. In more recent times it took part in the first Gulf War of 1991 and in Operation Telic (Invasion of Iraq) in 2003.

41 Squadron –Motto: Seek and Destroy

41 Squadron was stationed at Saint-Omer for a matter of days in October 1916 but returned later and stayed for August and September of 1918. They flew the FE8 and SE5A. A double cross which forms part of the Coat-of-Arms of the town of Saint-Omer featured on many of their aircraft. It was approved by HM King George VI in February 1937. 41 Squadron featured greatly in the Battle of Britain fighting against many enemy aircraft that were taking off from the aerodromes around Saint-Omer. 41 Squadron formed part of No 13 group. In more recent times the Squadron took part in Operation Telic in Iraq. The squadron now flies Tornados, Jaguars and Harriers.

16 Squadron Motto: Operta aperta: Hidden Things are revealed

No 16 was formed from the amalgamation of 2 and 6 Squadrons on Wednesday 10th February 1915 at Saint-Omer. It pioneered the use of 'wireless radio' to report enemy troop movements and played an important role in reporting such activity at frontline hotspots such as at Neuve Chappelle, Loos, Somme and Ypres. Like many of the other squadrons 16 Squadron was originally equipped with RE5, Vickers FB5 and Martinsyde aircraft. During World War Two 16 Squadron flew many reconnaissance sorties prior to D-Day and was finally disbanded at RAF Coltishall in 2005. The badge shows two keys, one in gold and one in black. Both symbolize the unlocking of enemy secrets, the gold representing day and the black by night. The regiment flag today hangs in one of the side chapels off the nave in the Cathedral of Saint-Omer.

16 Squadron colours as seen in the Cathedral of Saint-Omer © Photo Jonathan Caton

The two squadrons below deserve mention as they out of all the squadrons stationed here remained for the longest period of time. They are:

4 Squadron Motto: In futurum videre : To see into the future

Flying their Shorthorn, BE2 and RE8 aircraft, 4 Squadron was based in Saint-Omer between the 12th October 1914 and 21st April 1915. The Squadron returned towards the end of the war from the 16th April 1918 to the 18th September 1918. Their badge shows a red and black sun signifying the squadron's commitment to day and night operations whilst the bolt of lightning refers to the squadron's early role of wireless telephony for artillery co-operation. 4 Squadron operated out of Saint-Omer for 6 months in 1918 flying RE8s.

12 Squadron Motto: Leads the Field

The Squadron was based in Saint-Omer between 6th September 1915 and 28th February 1916 flying BE2, Bristol Scout, Morane, RE5 and RE7 aircraft. The squadron badge depicts a fox and is reference to the period (1926) that the squadron flew the 'Fairey Fox'. They were the only squadron to do so and were justly proud. 12 Squadron was nicknamed the 'Shiny Twelfth' on account of the Fox's shiny nose cowling. The motto is in reference to their daylight bombing development. Two pilots from this squadron were awarded the first VC's of World War II to an aircrew after their bravery in bombing a major bridge over the Albert Canal in France in May 1940 (Flight Officer Garland and Observer Sergeant Gray). The squadron went on to fly Wellingtons, Lancasters and in 1946 Lincolns. Operation Telic in Iraq is one of the Squadrons most recent active role in a theatre of war.

Aside the Squadrons themselves I would like to focus on some of the individuals within the RFC who served at Saint-Omer. Amongst them are:

Sir David Henderson by Walter Stoneman, negative 1918

© *National Portrait Gallery, London*

Some sources consider Lieutenant General Commanding Officer Sir David Y. Henderson as the father of the RAF. From the inauguration of the RFC in 1912

Henderson campaigned hard for its autonomy fending off amalgamation plans by both the Army and Royal Naval Air Service (RNAS). Adding considerable input into what is known as the 'Smuts Report' the Royal Air Force was created on 1st April 1918 after the RFC and RNAS were merged together.

David Henderson was one of four brothers born into a Scottish shipping dynasty on Monday 11th August 1862. At the age of fifteen he started his studies at the University of Glasgow specializing in Engineering. He never graduated however, instead choosing a career in the army. He entered Sandhurst and joined the Argyll and Sutherland Highlanders in 1883.

His military career was a successful one and he took part in campaigns in China, South Africa, Ceylon and France. His courage and bravery was noted in Dispatches during the South African War and the siege of Ladysmith. After this episode he was promoted to Lieutenant Colonel.

By this time Henderson was developing a keen interest in military intelligence and advancing the techniques for collating it. He served under Lord Kitchener in 1902 as Director of Military Intelligence and between 1904 and 1907 he wrote two books on the subject: "Field Intelligence: Its Principles and Practice" and "Reconnaissance".

His passion for intelligence gathering was to prove highly useful for his appointment as Head of the RFC in France at the outbreak of the First World War. He became the oldest Pilot in the Corps successfully gaining his wings at the age of 49. Due to his considerable commitments both as Head of the RFC and in his intellectual capacity to developing further the methods of intelligence gathering Henderson relinquished control of the RFC in favour of Brigadier General Hugh Trenchard in August 1915.

Henderson survived the war and died in Geneva on Wednesday 17th August 1921 surviving his son, Captain Ian Henderson who perished in a flying accident in June 1918. Henderson Senior stayed in the public eye right up until his death organizing amongst others things the League of the Red Cross Societies. During his life he was made a Knight Commander of the Order of the Bath and Knight Commander of the Royal Victorian Order. In addition, he did graduate finally from the University of Glasgow on 24th June 1920 when he received an Honourable LLD (Doctor of Laws).

Brigadier General Hugh M Trenchard, GCB, OM, GCVO, DSO

Hugh Montague Trenchard, 1st Viscount Trenchard after John Singer Sargent, collotype 1919 © National Portrait Gallery, London

Hugh Montague Trenchard was a Somerset man born in Taunton on Thursday 3rd April 1873. His ascendancy to the top echelons of the RAF would have been a surprise to him let alone to those around him had his early achievements been the sole indicator. Trenchard came from a military family, both parents being descendants of relatives serving in the Army or Navy. Trenchard did not excel particularly well at school and in fact barely passed his entrance exams into the Royal Scots Fusiliers. He did however excel at rugby and other outdoor pursuits namely hunting. Once commissioned, Trenchard was sent to India. Here he eclipsed his fellow officers in shooting and won for the Regiment the All India Rifle Championship of 1894. The fact that Trenchard did not descend from a wealthy family who could pay for the Army's more expensive field sport pursuits did not deter him in setting up a battalion Polo team which despite its lack of tradition and experience held its own against more traditionally Polo orientated regiments. During one of these matches occurred his first meeting with Winston Churchill with whom he crossed mallets. It was during this time that Trenchard earned the nickname of 'the Camel' for despite his sporting prowess, which was held in high regard by his fellow officers, it was felt that he lacked some of the social graces becoming of an officer: he barely spoke and hardly drank – just like our humped friend.

Trenchard saw little action in India which disappointed him but he used his time wisely becoming an avid reader particularly of military biographies – at last he was able to shake off some of his low academic esteem. From India, through his sporting connections and by pulling strings, Trenchard received a commission to go to fight in the Second Boer War in South Africa. Here Trenchard was given the responsibility of forming and training a Mounted Unit within the Royal Scots Fusiliers. This done they proved to be an efficient fighting unit up against a determined and competent opponent – The Boers, who were natural horsemen. During one skirmish Trenchard was lucky to come away with his life. A bullet ripped into his chest destroying a lung and leaving him partially paralysed. Trenchard was invalided out of service and sent back to England to recuperate.

Here Trenchard descended to his lowest ebb but was saved due to the generosity of Lady Dudley who saw to it that the young officer had the financial means to recuperate in Switzerland where it was felt that the clean air would surely aid his recovery. It was here rather bizarrely that Trenchard regained full mobility after being involved in a serious bobsleigh accident.

On his return to England Trenchard dismissed concerns over his fitness and instead volunteered for a second tour of duty in South Africa. After peace was declared in May 1902 he debated whether to quit the army or not. He was persuaded to remain in service on meeting General Kemball who had been appointed by the War Office to recruit for the Southern Nigerian Regiment. He took up the position of Deputy Commandant with the condition that he would personally lead all regimental exercises. Whilst in Nigeria Trenchard was awarded the Distinguished Services Order for his part in defeating the Ibo tribesmen of the Bende Onitsha region who had killed and eaten a British doctor. Having beaten the tribesmen in battle Trenchard set about building roads through the jungle using his considerable human resource called 'locals'.

Trenchard returned to England after he caught a particularly unpleasant illness - 'Blackwater Fever' – a rather severe form of malaria resulting in many cases in kidney failure then death. The year was 1906. Having recovered he returned to Nigeria as Commandant of the Southern Nigerian Regiment. This time he established strong trading links with the Munshi Tribe and also became a part-time sales negotiator for Harrods Department store in London setting up trading deals on their behalf in Nigeria.

Trenchard was again dogged by health problems. This time it was a rather nasty liver abscess so he was shipped back to England in the early part of 1910. This illness took some months to bring under control and it was not until October that same year that he was able to join the Royal Scots Fusiliers in Derry in Northern Ireland. He was reduced to rank of Major and peacetime life greatly frustrated the ambitious Trenchard. It was by now 1912 and he had fallen out with his commanding officer Colonel Stuart and was actively seeking other postings elsewhere without success.

A new chapter was soon to open for him in the form of a letter that he received from a fellow Officer and friend Captain Eustace Loraine which advocated that Trenchard must learn to fly. Obviously liking the notion (and I am sure that Trenchard was fully aware of the development of the aeroplane since Blériot had crossed the Channel three years earlier) he set about nagging his commanding officer to allow him to go and train to become a pilot. Trenchard, in terms of age for a trainee Pilot was right up there with the senior citizens. He was thirty-nine years old and the limit was forty. However he was successful in his application and acquired his 'Wings' after only sixty four minutes in the air. This however did not mean that he was an exceptional pilot; in fact if truth be told, he was quite the opposite. Trenchard's talents lay in being able to create opportunities, organise and implement procedures and it was not long before he was assigned a key administrative role in Central Flying School. He enforced the importance of map reading skills, mechanics and signalling for trainee pilots.

With the outbreak of the First World War Trenchard was promoted to Officer Commanding the wing of the Royal Flying Corps.

Trenchard worked closely with David Henderson whom we met earlier and was responsible for creating new RFC Squadrons to satisfy demand. A target of sixty Squadrons was initially set by Kitchener. This Trenchard achieved. By December 1916 there were 106 frontline Squadrons and 95 reserve and Training Squadrons.

Due to the demands placed on Henderson in France it was recommended by the latter and approved by Lord Kitchener that Trenchard should take over as head of the RFC. He stepped into the role on Wednesday 25th August 1915 as Brigadier General Officer Commanding the RFC in the Field.

Trenchard worked differently to Henderson preferring, to focus on maintaining a strong supply chain, attending to the small details that would enable his wing Commanders to work more efficiently and finally to encourage a more aggressive approach to combat. This included his belief that strategic Bombing was an effective way of subduing an enemy.   Trenchard's success in this role would not have been possible had it not been for the stoic work put in by his Intelligence Officer Maurice Baring.

Trenchard survived the war and was significantly involved in the future shaping of the RAF, so much so in fact that more sources than not credit him as being the father of the RAF. Trenchard went on after the Armistice to become Air Marshal of the RAF and oversaw the creation of the RAF Cadet College at Cranwell and also the Aircraft Apprentice scheme which supplied the RAF with vital ground crew. He was also responsible for the introduction of the short service commission and the creation of the University Air Squadron.

On New Year's Day 1927 Trenchard was promoted to the highest rank of the RAF – Marshal of the Royal Air Force at the age of 54. He remained in this position for three years to the day he retired out of the RAF on the 1st January 1930.

Retirement was a word that did not compute to someone like Trenchard and after a brief spell as a Director for the Goodyear Tire and Rubber Company he accepted the position of Metropolitan Police Commissioner. Here Trenchard in typical fashion set about making changes – one of them being the creation of the Police College at Hendon which took charge of its first intake in 1934.

Trenchard remained deeply loyal to the RAF and became its first peer in the House of Lords on his appointment as the Baron of Wolfton in Dorset in 1934. He travelled widely on the back of his Directorships of various companies including one visit to Germany in 1937 where he was entertained by the Head of the German Luftwaffe - Herman Goering. It has been noted that Goering remarked to Trenchard that "one day Germany will make the whole world tremble" to which Trenchard retorted that Goering "must be off his head".

Trenchard throughout his career spoke his mind and was always highly audible if he had a point of view. His period as head of the RFC in Saint-Omer shaped many of his opinions governing tactics in adopting offensive rather defensive action and administration for a future RAF. At the outbreak of World War Two he was asked to take up several posts which he declined for various reasons, one being a lack of tact! Instead he passed the war as a much-respected self-appointed General Inspector of RAF stations throughout the many theatres of war. Before his death at the age of 83 in 1956 he created with his old adversary Hugh Dowding the Anglo-American Memorial in St Paul's Cathedral, London and the Battle of Britain Chapel in Westminster Abbey and it is here that his ashes rest.

Now that we have read about some of the lives of those who commanded the RFC here are some notable RFC Personnel stationed at one time or another at Saint-Omer.

Captain John Aidan Liddell in uniform © Peter Daybell

Liddell found his way to the RFC via the Battalion of Princess Louise's Argyll and Sutherland Highlanders whom he joined before the start of hostilities in 1912. His apparent nickname of "Oozy" was on account of his constant tampering with engines (28). He spent many months in the trenches where his leadership qualities were noted in dispatches and also led to him being awarded the Military Cross in February 1915. We are able to glimpse the respect he held in regard to his fellow soldiers where one Private

Alexander McCullum of B company wrote in his diary of Liddell: "We have a splendid officer in charge of the guns, one of those men who would give the faintest-hearted confidence. May he be spared to see us all safely through the lot, for you have no idea what it means to lose confidence in your superior". However the horrors and stresses of trench warfare took their toll on a naturally frail Liddell and he was sent back to England to regain his health. At this point he decided that he could best serve his country by joining the RFC and on Saturday 24th July 1915 he joined No 7 squadron at Saint-Omer. Seven days later, on Saturday 31st July he was assigned a reconnaissance sortie and aircraft RE5 2457 - a 2 seater with his observer 2nd Lt Roland H Peck. It was to be his last sortie.

Captain J A Liddell's RE5 that he gallantly nursed back to safety after being fatally wounded.
He was awarded the VC for his outstanding courage. © Peter Daybell

The sortie was to take them over Ostend, Bruges, Ghent, Audenarde and Heesteert. They were attacked over Bruges at 5000 ft by an enemy aircraft which to this day remains a mystery as to its identity, and Liddell and his plane came off the worse. Liddell blacked out and spun out of control for 3000 ft. His right leg and thigh had been shattered in the hail of bullets and much of his cockpit ripped away. It was at this moment of most certain death for him and the conscious Peck that Liddell somehow revived himself and took stock and control of their ghastly situation. Loosing blood in a steady relentless flow coupled with blackouts caused by bouts of nauseating agony, Liddell made course for the safety of their lines. This took an unimaginable thirty minutes. Coupled with this was the necessity for considerable skill and resolve to control an aircraft that had been badly damaged. Liddell managed it but the severity of his injuries finally led to his death some weeks later on Monday 31st August – St Aidan's Day. His mother, Emily Liddell was given special dispensation to be at his bedside at the time of his death in La Panne in Belgium. He is reputed to have said "Mummy, I want to go home" to which she replied "You are going home sonny". He was awarded the Victoria Cross eight days before his death. He was the third of nineteen airmen to receive the VC during the entirety of World War One. Such was the respect and popularity he had gained in his short life his body was taken back to England where he had a full requiem mass at the Church of the Immaculate Conception, Farm Street officiated by the Rector of his old school, Father Bodkin of Stonyhurst College, Lancashire. He is interned in the churchyard at Basingstoke Church. For further reading on Captain Aidan Liddell I thoroughly recommend the extensive study made by Peter Daybell in his book '*With a Smile and a Wave: The Life of Captain Aidan Liddell VC MC.*'

Air Marshall William Avery "Billy" Bishop V.C., C.B., DSO & Bar, MC, DFC, ED

Major Billy Bishop and pilots from 85 Squadron © Imperial War Museum, London

Major Billy Bishop as he was at the time when he commanded 85 Squadron "the Flying Foxes" for a brief stay at Saint-Omer between 11th June and 5th July 1918. Bishop had a fearsome reputation and was a highly successful Ace with 72 victories which made him the highest scoring Canadian Ace if not top Ace of the British Empire. He transferred from the 7th Mounted Canadian Rifles at the start of the war after becoming sick of the horror of trench warfare. Bishop is reputed to have said "...it's clean up there! I'll bet you don't get any mud or horseshit on you up there. If you die, at least it would be a clean death." (29). Bishop was a gifted aerial photographer and in January 1916 was the Observer for Pilot Roger Neville flying an R.E.7 Reconnaissance aircraft from nearby Boisdinghem airfield. Bishop survived a crash in which his knee was badly damaged and recuperated back in Canada. He returned to frontline service in March 1917 as a Pilot attached to 60 Squadron based near Arras. It was a less than impressive return to operational duties because he had the misfortune of crash landing his aircraft in front of a visiting General, General John Higgins who strongly suggested that Bishop be sent back to England to attend Flying School. It was only due to the insistence of the 60 Squadron CO, Major Alan Scott that Bishop remained where he was. Literally the next day Bishop claimed his first victory. His tally rose rapidly after he made many 'lone-wolf' sorties deep into enemy territory. Ace status of 'five' victories was achieved on 8th April 1917 and to celebrate his nose cone was painted blue as was the norm for marking an Ace. His rapid rise of victories did not go unnoticed by the Germans who gave him the nickname "Hell's Handmaiden" and one Squadron put a price on his head. On 2nd June 1917 Bishop carried out a lone attack on a German airfield where he shot down three of the enemy who were trying to take off and destroyed several more on the ground. This action saw him awarded the Victoria Cross in July. The Canadian Government were keen to 'preserve' Bishop who had become somewhat of a Canadian National treasure and with great reluctance Bishop left France and relinquished his command of the 85 Squadron which passed to the much celebrated English Ace Major "Mick" Mannock. Aside his VC, Bishop was awarded the Distinguished Flying Cross, Distinguished Service Order and Distinguished Service Order Bar. Bishop was appointed an Honorary Air Marshall of the Canadian Air Force in 1938 with the responsibility of recruitment. He died peacefully in September 1956 in Palm Beach, Florida.

Pilots and ground crew of 85 Squadron at Saint-Omer aerodrome on 21ˢᵗ June 1918. In front left to right are Lt A.S.Cunningham-Ried, Capt M.C.Mcgregor, Lt D.C.Inglis (who accompanied Mick Mannock on his last sortie), Lt L.H.Callahan, Lt E.W. Spings, Baker (Acting CO), Canning, Daniel, Capt S.B.Horn, Carruthers, Capt A.C. Randall, Brown, Lt W.H.Longton, Lt J.Dymund, Capt G.D.Brewster, Herbert, Dickson, Cushing, Abbot and Capt Ross (Recording Officer)

© Imperial War Museum, London

Major Edward Corringham 'Mick' Mannock VC, DSO and two Bars, MC and Bar

Major 'Mick' Mannock is often referred to as the Ace of the Aces of the British Empire despite discrepancy over the number of victories credited to him which range between 51 and 71. Mannock took command of No 85 Squadron from "Billy" Bishop on Friday 5ᵗʰ July 1918. It has to be said that Mannock did not like Saint-Omer and is recorded as describing it as a 'nasty town, mainly composed of estaminets, old women, and dirty – very dirty children' (30). In comparison to the average age of his fellow Pilots he was advanced in years and handicapped by impaired sight in his left eye after suffering from amoebic infestation when ten years old. He went on to become one of the most respected pilots and aerial tacticians of the First World War. He developed the strategy of pilots flying as a unit and wherever possible utilizing his cardinal rule: "Fly always above, seldom on the same level and never below...the enemy must be surprised and attacked at a disadvantage, if possible with superior numbers so the initiative was with the patrol. The combat must continue until the enemy has admitted his inferiority, by being shot down or running away."

His route to the RFC was via the Royal Medical Corps and the Royal Engineers. He transferred to the RFC in August 1916. Due to a completely understandable and horrific phobic fear of being burned to death in his aircraft he always flew with a revolver at his side. He is quoted as saying "The other fellows all laugh at me for carrying a revolver. They think I'm going to shoot down a machine with it, but they're wrong. The reason I bought it was to finish myself as soon as I see the first signs of flames. They'll never burn me."

Mannock was an inspirational leader who was hugely missed and who it might be suggested was going through a breakdown at the time of his death. It was a death that his fellow flying officer Lt D C Inglis describes thus: "Falling in behind Mick again we made a couple of circles around the burning wreck and then made for home. I saw Mick start to kick his rudder, then I saw a flame come out of his machine; it grew bigger and bigger. Mick was no longer kicking his rudder. His nose dropped slightly and he went into a slow right-hand turn, and hit the ground in a burst of flame. I circled at about twenty feet but could not see him, and as things were getting hot, made for home and managed to reach our outposts with a punctured fuel tank. Poor Mick ...the bloody bastards had shot my Major down in flames"

The News of the World reported the loss as follows:

FAMOUS AIRMAN MISSING

Major Edward Mannock, R.A.F., "who had brought 58 German machines, is reported missing. He was last seen fighting over the German lines on July 20, and soon afterwards his machine was noticed to be falling in flames." Major Mannock has had a distinguished career since he joined the Royal Flying Corps 18 months ago. He rapidly became one of our foremost flyers, and when Canada's great aerial fighter, Major Billy Bishop, returned to the Dominians some months ago he succeeded Major Bishop in command of his squadron. Major Mannock's record of 58 machines down dates up to a month ago. When war broke out Major Mannock was in Turkey, and, coming home through Bulgaria, joined the R.A.M.C., attaining the rank of sergeant. Then he obtained a commission in the Royal Flying Corps, and although 30 years of age proved as skilful in the art of downing Huns as our youngest dare-devils. Major Mannock possesses the D.S.O. and M.C., each with two bars. Major Mannock is a nephew of Mr J.P. Mannock, a well-known billiard player of the time, and a native of London.

The News of the World, Sunday, 4th August, 1918

His father was presented with his son's VC at Buckingham Palace in July 1919. Mannock's body was never recovered and his name is commemorated on the RFC Memorial to the missing at the Faubourgs d'Amiens CWGC in Arras. A plaque commemorating this brave pilot can also be found in Canterbury Cathedral.

Major Cyril Newall GCB, OM, GCMG, CBE, AM

Cyril Louis Norton Newall was born on the 15th February 1886. He was a natural leader. Newall undertook considerable danger to himself along with Corporal Driver in evacuating from a burning munitions supply store at Saint-Omer aerodrome red-hot incendiary bombs in January 1916. Both men were burned, blackened but tireless in their successful efforts in averting great danger and damage to the surrounding area. Newall and Corporal Driver were both decorated, Newall receiving the Albert Medal. Newall commanded 12 Squadron in 1915-16. During World War II Newall was promoted to Air

Chief Marshall and from February 1941 to June 1946 was Governor General of New Zealand.

Captain Cecil Arthur Lewis MC

Cecil Arthur Lewis was based here briefly in March 1916. An Ace with eight victories which he won between May and June 1917 he flew a variety of aircraft with numerous squadrons. He was awarded the Military Cross for his courageous actions during the Battle of the Somme. After the war he co-founded the BBC in 1922 and went on to become a successful writer, director and producer. One of his novels is called Sagittaruis Rising. This aviation classic was adapted as a screenplay starring Christopher Plummer amongst other notables in the film "Aces High". Lewis, George Bernard Shaw, Ian Dalrymple and W.P. Lipscomb received Oscars for their screen adaptation of Shaw's play "*Pygmalion*" in 1938. George Bernard Shaw described him as "This prince of pilots has had the most charmed life in every sense of the word. He is a thinker, a master of words and a bit of a poet."

Major Cyril Marconi "Billy" Crowe DFC, MC

Commander of the 85 Squadron flying SE 5's from Saint-Omer in the last months of the war. An ace with 15 victories he was awarded the Distinguished Flying Medal and Military Cross. He pioneered new combat tactics for the S.E.5 called 'Dive and Climb'. Amazingly he survived the war. I say 'amazingly' because he had the good fortune of escaping without injury an incident on Monday 7th May 1917 when his goggles were literally shot off his face whilst in combat. He became a Wing Commander in World War Two and died in 1974.

Major Geoffrey Hilton 'Beery' Bowman MC Bar, DSO, DFC

Born in Manchester on 2nd May 1891 he was the son of George (a physician) and Mary Bowman. Major Bowman joined the RFC in March 1916 from the Royal Warwickshire Regiment which he joined as a Lieutenant at the start of the war. His first Squadron was No 29 and it might be said that he was very lucky to be alive after claiming his first victory over a German 'Roland' aircraft. It was bought down in a head on collision. His score mounted after joining 56 Squadron which flew SE5's. His life was spared again on Wednesday 5th September when the spars on his wings broke causing him to crash land. He was obliged to transfer to 41 Squadron as Commander on 9th February 1918 where his score rose further. He was now considered valuable property of the RAF who ordered that "Major Bowman is forbidden to leave the ground on any pretext whatsoever, without the personal permission of the GOC, II Brigade". When the war finished Bowman had scored 32 victories. He remained in the RAF until 1934 but was recalled at the outbreak of World War II. He left the RAF permanently in December 1941. His nickname 'Beery' came from his rosy complexion. He died on 25th March 1970.

Many of the servicemen stationed at Saint-Omer would have been familiar with an affectionate song that was sung here celebrating their fondness for the aerodrome and town aside of course Mick Maddock. The words to the song have been cast in bronze on a plaque and are on permanent show at the British Services Memorial at Saint-Omer Aerodrome.

OMER DROME

I've got a windy feeling round my heart

And it's time that we went home!

I've got a great big longing to depart

Somewhere back to Omer Drome

Huns are diving at my tail

Wing Up – Gee – I've got a gale

Guns are jamming

Pilots are damning

Archies bursting all around us

And observers say

Ain't it time that we came down?

So won't you splitass back

Along the track

To my dear old Omer town?

Traditionally sung to the tune of Old Kentucky

The evocative bronze relief at the British Services Memorial dedicated to the airmen
based at Saint-Omer during the First World War erected by Cross and Cockade,
the First World War Aviation Historical Society in 2004 © Photo Jonathan Caton

The history of the RFC and Saint-Omer is a major undertaking in itself and I am sincerely grateful for the help and source material that I received from the Department of Research at RAF Hendon and Air Commodore Peter Dye who has written on this subject: if you are interested in learning more I strongly recommend as a starting point reading his study that is printed in the Cross and Cockade International Journal Vol 35 No 2 2004 'The Royal Flying Corps & Royal Air Force at Saint-Omer'.

It is important to point out that just below the airfield off route des Bruyères (D928) is the Commonwealth War Graves Commission (CWGC) Souvenir Cemetery where more than one hundred airmen lie and in this respect it is the largest grouping of RFC RAF Personnel in Europe. Amongst the 'Glorious Dead' that lie here as an ever present reminder of their sacrifice are seven World War One Aces and here are their stories.

Captain David Sydney Hall MC

David Sydney Hall joined the RFC via the Argyll and Sutherland Highlanders. He was awarded the Military Cross for conspicuous gallantry and devotion to duty whilst serving with 57 Squadron and flying an Airco D.H.4. This aircraft was the only British plane designed by the Americans. It earned itself the macambre nickname of 'the Flying Coffin' on account that its fuel tank was situated between the pilot and the observer. Hall and Observer Edward Hartigan shot down four enemy aircraft (two each).

The London Gazette of the time reported the occasion.

"While leading back his formation of five machines from a bombing raid he was attacked on eight different occasions by numerous enemy scouts. He himself shot down one in flames and another out of control, while his observer shot down two in flames. He has at all times, completed the task allotted to him, and set a splendid example."

Supplement to *The London Gazette*, 6 April 1918 (30614/4215)

Captain Hall and 2nd Lt Hartigan

Captain Hall and his Observer, Edward Patrick Hartigan went missing after taking off from Saint-Omer at 09h45 en route for what is now known as the first battle of Cambrai on Tuesday 20th November 1917.

Edward Partick Hartigan joined the RFC on Sunday 1st October 1916 via the Battalion of the Royal Munster Fusiliers. He was an Observer with the rank of Flying Officer. He joined 57 Squadron and his Pilot Officer was Captain David Sydney Hall who is buried next to him. The pair succeeded in scoring five victories in October 1917 but were reported as missing on the first day of the Battle of Cambrai on Tuesday 20th November 1917. Confirmation of their deaths was confirmed on the discovery of their crashed D.H.4 A7586 at Les Alleux. Captain Hall is buried at plot IV.F.10 and Lt Hartigan at Plot No: IV.F.9

Sergeant John Cowell DCM, MM and Bar

John Cowell was born in Limerick in 1889. He started the war as a Sapper (Combat Engineer) with the 12th Field Company of the Royal Engineers and then joined the RFC as a mechanic and then as an observer/gunner for 20 Squadron. He scored 16 victories mostly with the FE2B but ended up flying the Bristol Fighter. He was shot down and killed in his Bristol Fighter E2471 near Ypres on Tuesday 30th July 1918 along with his observer Corporal Charles William Hill by Lieutenant Frederick von Röth of Jasta 16b. Röth killed himself on New Year's Eve of the same year on account of Germany's defeat. Sergeant Cowell is buried in Souvenir Plot No: V.D.19

Below is a colourful account by US Pilot Frederick Libby describing the risks pilots and observers took when flying the FE2B as Cowell had done so before changing to the Bristol Fighter F2B:

"When you stood up to shoot [in the F.E.2b], all of you from the knees up was exposed to the elements. There was no belt to hold you. Only your grip on the gun and the sides of the nacelle stood between you and eternity. Towards the front of the nacelle was a hollow steel rod

with a swivel mount to which the gun was anchored. This gun covered a huge field of fire forward. Between the observer and the pilot a second gun was mounted, for firing over the F.E.2b's upper wing to protect the aircraft from rear attack ... Adjusting and shooting this gun required that you stand right up out of the nacelle with your feet on the nacelle coning [sic]. You had nothing to worry about except being blown out of the aircraft by the blast of air or tossed out bodily if the pilot made a wrong move. There were no parachutes and no belts. No wonder they needed observers."

2nd Lt Percy Griffith Jones

Lieutenant Percy Jones was the son of Griffith and Annie Jones of The Chalet, Mold, Flint, North Wales. Born in 1889 and 25 years old at the outbreak of the war he joined the Royal Engineers whom he stayed with until November 1917. At this point he transferred to the RFC as was common practice for many serving in engineering regiments and joined 2 Squadron. On 27th April 1917 he was attached to 20 Squadron and between the 15th May and 2nd July 1917 he claimed five victories. He was killed on Tuesday 2nd July 1918 aged 29 and is buried at plot V.C.38

2nd Lt George Hubert Kemp

Aged 17 at the start of the war George Hubert Kemp started his military career with the 15th Battalion of the Durham Light Infantry. He joined the RFC as a 2nd Lt attached to 20 Squadron on Sunday 26th May 1918 and quickly scored 12 victories between this date and his death aged just 20 on Saturday 1st June 1918. He flew as an observer in a Bristol F.2b with his pilot Lt W M Thomson who survived.

Captain Arthur Norbury Solly and Lt Donald Yalden Hay

Born in 1894 Arthur Norbury Solly was an experienced pilot who at the time of his death on Tuesday 11th August 1917 had been credited with 9 victories. He was the son of Major Ernest Solly and Mary Alice Solly of Strathlea, Harrogate. He attended Rugby

School before going on to Gonville and Caius College, Cambridge. Solly found his way to the RFC via the 19th Battallion Royal Fusiliers Manchester Regiment. On entering the RFC as a Flight Commander he was attached to 20 and 23 Squadrons. His gravestone is shared by his observer Lieutenant Donald Yalden Hay to whom he was a great friend. Both men died when the wing on their Bristol F 2.B A7108 collapsed and caused the aircraft to crash on take-off from Saint-Omer aerodrome at 10:50am 11 August 1917.

Details kindly supplied by The Sole Society and by Peter van den Heuvel.

2nd Lt Albert Edward Wear

2nd Lt Albert Edward Wear was 19 years old when the First World War broke out. He enlisted and joined the Royal Fusiliers transferring to the RFC 20 Squadron in 1917. He notched up 9 victories in his Bristol Fighter A6448 often flying with Australian Ace Lt Cecil Roy Richards MC. The pair took part in a fight against 'The Red Baron' Manfred von Richthofen on Friday 6th July 1917 when the Baron was shot down and wounded. Richards was shot down near Le Quesnoy on the Sunday 19th August and captured by Ernst Hess of Jasta 28. Lieutenant Wear was killed in an accident on Tuesday 11th September.

It is not possible in this book to name every soldier, airmen, doctor, nurse, orderly, padre or partisan who died and is interned here in Saint-Omer during WW1. However I would urge a visit to the Souvenir Commonwealth War Graves Cemetery (CWGC) at Longuenesse. Every graveyard tells stories and the CWGC cemeteries are no different. Once in, one is immediately sensitive to the ambience of peace and calm that they never fail to exude, whether the entrance is via a grand portal or a simple gate. You are enveloped in an atmosphere separate from our hectic and busy lives. The neat rows of white Portland stone graves, impeccably manicured grass and carefully selected plants and flowers never cease to impress and move whether the number interned there be a few clustered together as can be seen at St-Martin-au-Laërt or in their thousands as seen at the CWGC Etaples. The Souvenir Cemetery of Longuenesse is no different in any of these respects. The road is the busy D928 but the large heavy gates form an aesthetic and physical barrier from this. In front of you on a gentle slope downwards lie 3 438 men and women from the First and Second World Wars.

The CWGC 'Souvenir' Cemetery at Longuenesse © Photo Jonathan Caton

'Souvenir' was designed by Sir Hubert Baker who was one of three leading architects of the day chosen to design the graveyards. The other two were Sir Edmund Lutyens and Sir Reginald Blomfield. The horticultural experts of the Gardens of Kew – including one of the leading garden designers of the day, Gertrude Jekyl, - were also closely associated with advising the Commission over the issue of appropriate floral decoration with Rudyard Kipling providing his genius for poignant and precise use of the English language with the immortalised phrase "Their name liveth forevermore" (Book of Ecclesiasticus).

As previously explained it is not possible to list and name all these worthy men and women here let alone recount their admirable tales but in order to give you some idea of the numbers involved I have listed instead the names of the regiments that are represented here from WW1. In the First World War alone I have accounted for one hundred and one different British regiments. This is an enormous number and truly reflects the scale on which Kitchener's Volunteer and Regular armies were based. The WW1 regiments in this cemetery are as follows:

Argyl and Sutherland Highlanders, Army Cyclist Corps, Artist's Rifles, Border Regiment, Black Watch, Bedfordshire Regiment, Cambridgeshire Regiment, Cameronians (Scots Rifles), Cheshire Regiment, Connaught Rangers, Coldstream Guards, Devonshire Regiment, Durham Light Infantry, Duke of Wellington Regiment, Duke of Cornwall's Light Infantry, 4th Dragoon Guards, 6th Dragoon Guards, Dorsetshire Regiment, East Kent Regiment (The Buffs), East Lancashire Regiment, East Surrey Regiment, East Yorkshire Regiment, Essex Regiment, Gloucester Regiment, Gordon Highlanders, Grenadier Guards, Highland Light Infantry, Honourable Artillery Company, 10th Hussars, 20th Hussars, Irish Guards, King's Dragoon Guards, King's Liverpool Regiment, King's Royal Rifle Corps, King's Own Royal Irish Hussars, King's Own Scottish Borderers, King's Shropshire Light Infantry, King's Own Yorkshire Light Infantry, Lincolnshire Regiment, 3rd Battalion London Regiment Royal Fusiliers, 7th Battalion London Regiment, Leicestershire Regiment, 9th Lancers, 1st Life Guards, 2nd Life Guards, 22nd Battalion London Regiment, 24th Battalion London Regiment, London

Scottish Regiment, Loyal North Lancashire Regiment, Machine Gun Corps, Middlesex Regiment, Manchester Regiment, Norfolk Regiment, Northamptonshire Regiment, Northamptonshire Yeomanry, Northumberland Fusiliers, North Irish Horse Regiment, North Somerset Yeomanry, Notts and Derby Regiment, Oxford and Bucks Light Infantry, Post Office Rifles, PWO Civil Service Rifles, Queens, Queen's Bays, Queen's Own Oxfordshire Hussars, 4th Queen's Own Hussars, Royal Army Service Corps, Royal Army Vetinary Corps, Royal Berkshire Regiment, Royal Dublin Fusiliers, Royal Engineers, Royal Field Artillery, Royal Garrison Artillery, Royal Horse Guards, 19th Royal Hussars, Royal Inniskilling Fusiliers, Royal Irish Regiment, Royal Lancaster Regiment, XIIth Royal Lancers, Royal Munster Fusiliers, Royal Scots, Royal Scots Greys Regiment, Royal Sussex Regiment, Royal Warwickshire Regiment, Royal Welch Fusiliers, Royal West Kent Regiment, Seaforth Highlanders, Somerset Light Infantry, South Lancashire Regiment, South Staffordshire Regiment, South Wales Borderers, Suffolk Regiment, South Notts Hussars, Welch Regiment, Voluntary Aid Detachment (VAD Nurses), West Yorkshire Regiment, York and Lancaster Regiment, Wiltshire Regiment, Worcester Regiment and Yorkshire Regiment.

Also buried in this cemetery are many soldiers from the Commonwealth countries amongst those being the 3rd Regiment South African Infantry, a large number of Canadian soldiers from the 1st, 2nd, 3rd, 4th, 5th, 7th, 8th, 10th, 13th, 14th, 15th, 16th, 26th, 42nd, 43rd and 58th Canadian Infantry Regiments, Canadian Field Artillery, Princess Patricia's Canadian Light Infantry and soldiers from the 4th Canadian Mounted Rifles.

From Australia there are soldiers from the Australian Army Medical Corps, 2nd Australian Pioneers, and others from the 19th, 17th and 20th Battalions of the Australian Infantry. From New Zealand there are soldiers from the Maori Battalion, the NZ Canterbury Regiment, New Zealand Medical Corps and the New Zealand Rifle Brigade. No less important are those war dead of French, Belgian and German nationalities here from the First and Second World War.

There are some graves for those in the Chinese Labour Corps – a work force drafted in to carry out essential works such as road and rail repair, sandbag filling as well as trench digging.

A Medical Sergeant, Chinese Labour Corps 1918 by Adrian Hill

© Imperial War Museum, London

THE BLACKSMITH. CHINESE LABOUR CORPS.

No 5

A Blacksmith, Chinese Labour Corps 1918 by Adrian Hill

© Imperial War Museum, London

THE CARPENTER. CHINESE LABOUR CORPS.

No 4.

The Carpenter, Chinese Labour Corps 1918 by Adrian Hill

© Imperial War Museum, London

221

There is a plaque in the north transept of the Cathedral of Saint-Omer which commemorates the lives of those sacrificed from the member countries of the Commonwealth.

The plaque in the north transept of the Cathedral of Saint-Omer commemorating

the million lives of the men and women from the Commonwealth countries

whose lives were lost during the First World War. © Photo Jonathan Caton

After World War One Saint-Omer ceased to be the major garrison town it had once been. Indeed quite the opposite. What was left of the shattered French garrisons were now located in Calais and other towns aside Saint-Omer like Aire-sur-la-Lys in the area. Saint-Omer became the headquarters for the '*Centre Regional d'Instruction et de Ré-education Physique*' as well as the regional Military Recruiting Bureau. After the departure of the *8ème R.I.* in 1920 to Calais the only residing military presence was from the *6ème Régiment des Chasseurs* who were barracked here between 1923 and 1928. Saint-Omer retained the *Hôpital Militaire*.

After Britain and France declared war on Germany on Sunday 3rd September 1939 the reception of the news by the populace could not have been in more contrast to the 'jubilant' cries announcing the beginning of the First World War. The people of Saint-Omer were no different from those all over Europe – they did not want another war despite the obvious necessity for intervention. Indeed, Wagand the French Commander-in-Chief at the time summed up the situation by saying "we have gone to war with a 1918 army against a German army of 1939" (31). There are four hundred and two World War Two servicemen and women buried at Longuenesse Souvenir Cemetery and for the majority, death occurred either in 1940 coinciding with the end of the Battle of France and the withdrawal of the British and French armies from Dunkerque in Operation Dynamo or at the end of the war – Liberation in 1944 (for Saint-Omer) and 1945 for other parts of Europe. Between these two dates lay one thousand two hundred and forty five days of occupation of the town by the Nazi occupiers.

The town and surrounding area were overcome on Thursday 23rd May 1940 by the German Army 41st Corps. The British Green Howards amongst others tried to stall their advance wherever possible. One example took place at Watten where the bridge which crossed the Canal and River Aa was destroyed. Fierce struggles developed in obstructing the German advance to occupy the strategically important towns of Cassel and Hazebrouck –both not far from Saint-Omer. As Wagand predicted it was to no avail.

After the occupation began, Marshall Pétain signed an agreement with Germany in June 1940, to divide France into zones. From the outset the two most northern departments of France namely Nord, Pas-de-Calais came under the jurisdiction of the Military Governor of Brussels, the rest of occupied France came under the authority of the Military Governor of Paris. An initial 'forbidden-zone' was allocated to north western France but this was phased out in December 1941 and the Nord, Pas-de-Calais who were already experiencing a more inflexible and stringent occupation due to the geographic location of the area, were categorized as of March 1942 a 'forbidden zone'. In essence this restricted the movement and freedom of people and security was constantly tight and penalties stringent for offenders. On a more sinister note it meant the deportation of many people into forced labour camps. *L'Indépendant* newspaper reflects these harsh times as it became a communicator of severe dos and don'ts for the local French people. Another influential paper during this time was *La Voix du Nord*. This was for many a voice in the dark giving hope and coded messages to the Resistance. Listening to BBC Radio announcements was a clandestine activity and if discovered the penalty was death. There were many rules restricting the sale of goods and severe rationing was common. The fruits of heavy industry and manufacture continued in the North of France but the vast majority of produce was looted and sent back to Germany.

The poster below states clearly to the local people that they must report the sightings of any downed airmen, abandoned parachutes and report any activity connected with British military personnel or otherwise. Failure to comply meant death or deportation.

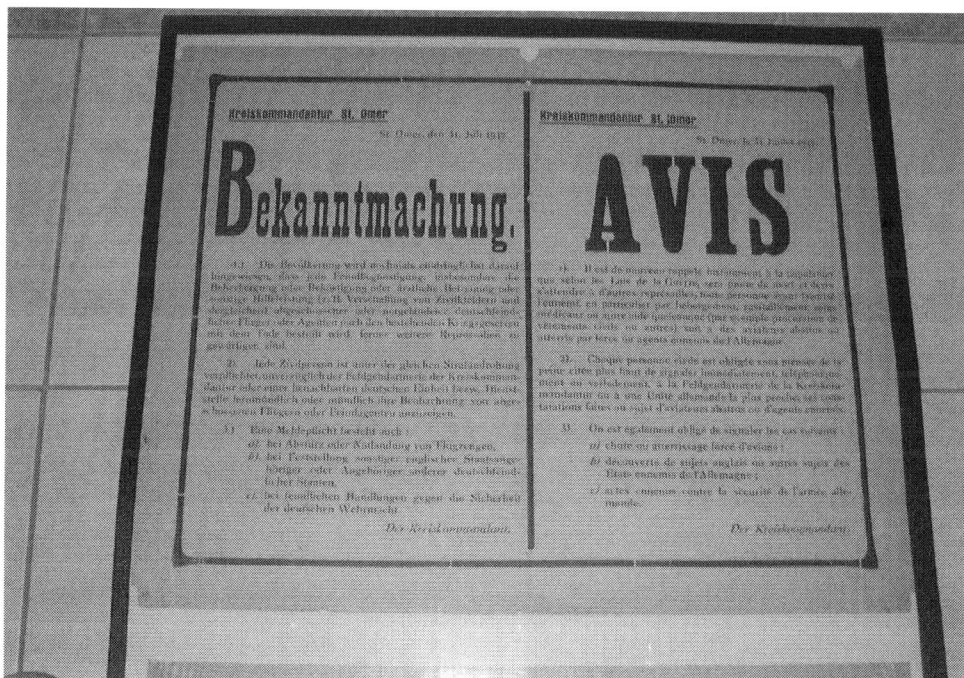

Copy of the German proclamation declaring the above. This poster was distributed widely in the area and issued in March 1941 Poster © Stéphane Milamon

Aside the German Army's considerable presence in the town, the Commandant's HQ being in *Place Victor Hugo* where the *Chambre of Commerce* offices now reside, the

Luftwaffe had many airbases scattered around the area including at the aerodrome of Saint-Omer and dotted in amongst the woods and marshes of Clairmarais. The bases around Saint-Omer were home to squadrons flying BF109 and BF110 fighters who were escorting the droves of Heinkel and Dornier bombers attacking Britain. The Germans were very good at disguising their airfields and Douglas Bader took great interest in this when given a personal tour of an airbase near Saint-Omer after his capture in 1941. The Luftwaffe commissioned the building of 'dummy' planes in wood and canvas as seen in the photo below.

Decoy planes made from wood and doped canvas designed to confuse Allied missions

© Stéphane Milamon

Saint-Omer itself was not a serious target for bombing by the Allies in comparison to many other cities and towns. It did not however go unscathed and was hit hard on many occasions particularly by allied missions targeting the airfields, Blockhaus d'Eperlecques and La Coupole. Despite this it is still incredulous that the town escaped with so few fatalities and damage. However there was one particular raid that caused devastation to the south eastern part of the town and resulted in a large loss of life. The day in question was Thursday 13th May 1943. It was a beautifully clear day. Whilst the people of Saint-Omer and its communes went about their business a formation of Boeing B17's from the 8th USAF took off from London and crossed over the Channel arriving in France above Le Touquet. There were fifty-eight Bombers escorted by one hundred and twenty-four Thunderbolt fighters. They met with no opposition. Their target was the aerodrome at the *Plateau des Bruyéres* in Longuenesse and La Coupole. The bomber crews were young and relatively inexperienced. They were over the target at 16h37 when they dropped their cargo of 73 tons of bombs in just under two minutes. The result was catastrophic - not for the Luftwaffe airfield below but for south eastern part of Saint-Omer notably *rue d'Arras, rue de Thérouanne* and *rue des Madeleines*. In those two minutes an estimated four hundred houses were destroyed. One hundred and fifteen people were killed instantly whilst around three hundred were wounded, many requiring amputations. A plea somehow got to London asking for more accuracy in bombing missions. The picture overleaf from the USAF archives shows the devastation.

USAF photo showing the devastation created by the raid on the 13th May 1943

Neg No SA 312 Saint-Omer 13.5.43 Print No 1 24655 Photo US Air Force, Montgomery,

Authorisation Yves Le Maner © Association Devoir de Mémoire

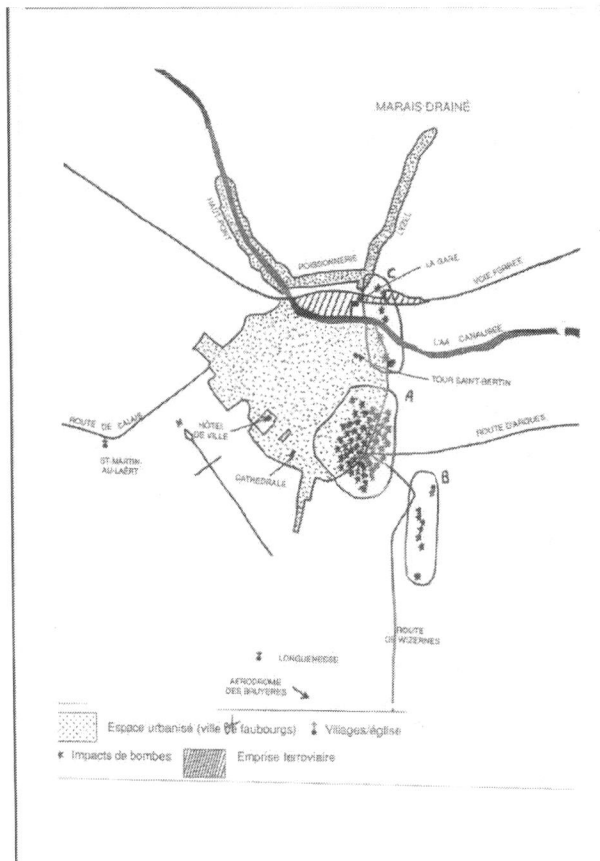

Local map showing precise area of damage within Saint-Omer

© Association Devoir de Mémoire

rue d'Arras after the raid with the Chapelle des Jésuites behind © Association Devoir de Mémoire

L'Audomarois: Home to Hitler's Vergeltungswaffen / Reprisal Weapons

Long before the start of the war in 1939 the Nazis were pioneering the research and development of balistic weapons. Amongst the thousands of scientists and engineers based at the isolated and top-secret military research centre at Peenëmunde were Dr Wernher von Braun, a civilian physicist and General Walter Dornberger. One of the results of this research was weapons known as the 'Reprisal' or 'V' - Vergeltungswaffen in German. There were three of them, two were missiles, the V1 and V2 and the third was a super gun resembling a massively enlarged torpedo tube that would enable Hitler to shell London from the coast of France. When these weapons finally materialised they were a very real threat and they brought terror to the daily lives of ordinary people who had to endure the day-to-day possibility that a 'V' weapon would destroy their home, killing and maiming anyone within the vicinity of the impact area.

The feelings of one A D Mitchell, a sailor in the Royal Navy is quite clear concerning the V1. He recounts on a visit home:

"...how different in 1944. The Terror of the buzz-bomb or V1 was in full swing. You could hear one coming. It seized you up inside. You waited for the motor to stop. It concentrated the mind, "please, please, keep going" you said (to yourself, of course). And then it would stop. We all looked at each other. Where would it land? And then the wonderful relief as it crunched onto some poor people. Night after night the people of London, Surrey and Kent endured this agony. And they say V2 was worse!

Next morning I addressed the assembled company. "I'm going back to sea, folks. It's safer there!" **A.D. Mitchell** (32)

The threat of the V super gun concerns the writer Evelyn Waugh so much so that he writes in his diary on the 13th November 1943:

"There is a great deal of talk at the moment about the rocket guns which the Germans are said to have set up in France, with a range to carry vast charges to London. This fear is seriously entertained in the highest quarters. I have accordingly given orders for the books I have been keeping at the Hyde Park Hotel to be sent to Piers Court. At the same time, I have

advocated my son coming to London. It would seem from this that I prefer my books to my son. I can argue that firemen rescue children and destroy books, but the truth is that a child is easily replaced, while a book destroyed is utterly lost; also a child is eternal; but most that I have a sense of absolute possession over my library and not over my nursery!" (33)

Back in France in l'Audomarois the misery that these weapons brought was also strongly felt by the wretched and unfortunate people forced to work round the clock, in conditions that beggar belief, not only in constructing them but also in building the concrete fortresses that would become their launch pads. And finally there is the consideration of the weapons themselves. The technology behind these projectiles of death was groundbreaking but extremely dangerous – they were very unstable. The 'blue prints' for them were highly sought after when the war ended and became a valuable prize for the allies on the liberation of the Blockhaus and La Coupole in 1944 as were the leading engineers. For example Von Braun went on to work for the Redstone program in Hunstville, Alabama after the war to help in the development of rocket technology.

In January 1943 engineers Fritz Gosslau and Robert Lusser presented the Nazi regime with their first 'V' projectile, the V1 commonly known as the Buzz bomb, Flying Bomb or Doodlebug on account of its insect-like sounding pulse engine when in flight. Hitler now needed bases from which to launch this monstrosity.

One of the major differences between the V1 and V2 was that the former required a horizontal launch pad. These 'pads' took the form of ramps. They were not small being a minimum of 42 metres and thus easily detectable from the air. The V1's also necessitated a whole host of other vehicles and personnel required for its launch. The forests of l'Audomarois provided excellent camouflage for these rather cumbersome metal pistes and the fervent activity going on around them.

There were operational launch sites at the following locations within l'Audomarois all with-in an eight mile radius of Saint-Omer: The Forest of Tournehem, Journy, Zudausques, Le Nieppe, Wisques, Bois d'Esquerdes, Nielles-les-Bléquin, Drionville, Bois de Longatte, Vaudringhem, Coubronne, Blanc-Pignon, Cauchie, Delettes, Enguinegatte, Bois Quartier, Bois de Renty, Vincly, Rebecques, Rimeux and Les Gros Bois. (34)

From the 13th June 1944 onwards the citizens of the 'Audomarois' would have been startled at the sound of the V1's firing up and accelerating up their pistes at 350 mph with the aid of a high pressurised steam and chemical catapult. The noise was distinctive and unnerving as we know from the account given by Seaman Mitchell. For those who took a look up at the sky would have been the first to see these lethal pilotless planes powered by the latest form of technology – the jet. What they were witnessing were the first waves of missile ever launched and many were destined for London and the South-East. English Heritage marks the site where the first V1 exploded on English soil, killing eight civilians on Thursday 13th June 1944 at the Mile End Grove railway bridge.

In all 22 384 V1 flying bombs were fired from a multitude of sites in Northern France between June 1944 and March 1945 at London and the South-East, Liege, Antwerp and Paris. Of this total 10 492 were fired at London and the south-east. They were famously inaccurate with 50% never reaching their targets however that did not reduce their high tally of mortalities and injuries. Over six thousand people died as a result of the V1 in London and the South-East with nearly eighteen thousand injured - many seriously.

With a top speed of 400mph the V1 came into range of some of the RAF and Allies' fastest fighters some of those being the Supermarine Spitfire, Hawker Tempest, Mustang III and Mosquito. To counteract the terror and fear that the people of London and the South-East were experiencing Churchill ordered the RAF and the Americans to designate some of its airpower to negate the threat from the V1. This strategy came under what was known as Operation Crossbow which was set up to tackle the threat of the German long-range weapons programme which included targeting the research and development centres of these weapons, the points of manufacture, transportation to and from the sights, their launch sites and finally to intercept the missiles once in flight. One squadron attached to the duties of Operation Crossbow was 501 Squadron. Its squadron leader at the time was Joseph Berry who in 1944 became one of the RAF's top scorers for shooting down V1's. David Watkins in his book '*Fear Nothing*' describes Churchill's instructions to Berry:

"I was called away yesterday and received instructions about the role of the 501 [Squadron] against the night intruders. It was said to me that these instructions came from the Prime Minister himself to the effect that the squadron must consider itself expendable and thus will take off to try to effect interception in every weather condition…even though all other squadrons are grounded, this, because it was felt that the threat of the V1 is so great that the people on the ground must at least 'hear' fighters airborne whenever there is a V1 warning. So the squadron will get airborne even if it is quite impossible to make any interception."

There were many pilots who put themselves at incredible risk and with amazing courage tried to destroy these 'V' weapons. Accurate gunnery under intense pressure was one thing. If that option failed consider this: four hundred miles an hour is incredibly fast. Imagine the skill and steady nerve that a pilot would require to draw alongside the hurtling projectile belching out intense heat and florescent flame in an attempt to nudge the fins using his own aircraft's wing tips to knock it off course as seen in the photo below. In the trade this is known as 'wing-tipping'.

A Supermarine Spitfire manoeuvring alongside a V1 ready to make 'contact'

© Imperial War Museum, London

A Spitfire tipping the gyros of a V1 to knock it off course

© Imperial War Museum, London

There are three pilots that I would like to bring to your attention. All three flew for the RAF, two British and one French - all three specialists in downing the V1. The first is the aforementioned Squadron Leader Joseph Berry.

Squadron Leader Joseph Berry outside the Ministry of Information Building (Senate House) on 7th September 1944. Later that day he recorded for the BBC his strategy for downing V1's. The photo was taken shortly before his death on 2nd October 1944. By kind permission of his widow Mrs Joyce Manser

Squadron Leader Joseph Berry shot down a total of sixty V1's out of which fifty-two and a half were destroyed in six weeks including seven in one sortie on Sunday 23rd July 1944. He flew the Hawker Tempest as seen overleaf.

Squadron Leader Joseph Berry DFC and 2 Bars.
Enemy Aircraft Destroyed - 3
Flying Bombs Destroyed - 60
501 Squadron, Bradwell Bay, Essex
October 2nd 1944.

Hawker Tempest V (Series II) EJ600, SD-F.

Graham Berry

Hunter of the V1 – The Hawker Tempest © Graham Berry

Berry gives us great insight into the strategy that he and doubtless many other pilots used for shooting down V1's. In a BBC radio broadcast of the Home Service's '*War Report*' recorded on the 7th September for the 9th September transmission Berry personally tells us that:

"We patrol at between 5 and 6000 feet, that's about 3000 feet higher than the path of the average flying bomb. The first thing we usually see is a small light rather hard to distinguish from a star coming in from the sea, then the search lights light up and point out the direction from which the bomb is coming. The guns go into action and we wait for the bombs that get through the gun belt, as soon as we spot a bomb that's run the gauntlet successfully we make a diving turn and go down after it, finishing our dive just behind the bomb and opening fire at a range of about 250 yards. The 'Doodlebug' doesn't go down easily; it will take a lot of punishment and you have to aim at the propulsion unit, that's the long stove pipe as we call it on the tail, if your range and aim are dead on you can see pieces flying off the stove pipe the big white flame at the end goes out and down goes the bomb. Sometimes it dives straight to earth,

237

but other times it goes crazy and gives a wizard display of aerobatics before finally crashing, Sometimes the bomb explodes in mid-air and the flash is so blinding that you can't see a thing for about 10 seconds, you hope to be the right way up when you are able to see again, because the explosion often throws the fighter about, and sometimes turns it upside down.

One bomb that I attacked caught fire, and started to dive onto a lighted aerodrome. I closed in behind and opened fire at about 100 yards giving it a long burst with my cannons, the bomb blew up much to the relief of the flying control officer who was watching it on the aerodrome. Fragments of the bomb were blown into my aircraft and one went into the air intake, jamming the throttle, which was almost wide open. I went home at full speed whether I liked it or not; fortunately I managed to get down safely."

He was awarded 'half' a victory for the action above. The extract above was given to me by the kind permission of Graham Berry. Squadron Leader Joseph Berry was shot down and killed on 2nd October of the same year.

The Nottingham Evening Post reported the news of his being classified as 'missing' as follows:

ACE V1 Killer is Missing

'Ace flying bomb killer Squadron Leader Joseph Berry D.F.C. and bar, aged 24, of Carlton, Nottinghamshire, who had destroyed 60, is reported missing, believed killed. While flying low over Holland, his plane was hit from a shot by a small gun and went down in flames. His last words over the radio telephone were: "Carry on chaps, I've had it."

Wing Commander Roland 'Bee' Beamont CDE, DSO, DFC. The Photo was taken when he was with 87 Squadron 1940. With kind permission of Newark Air Museum Archive ©

The second pilot expert in destroying the V1 was Wing Commander Roland 'Bee' Beamont. Surviving the Second World War he went on to play a major part in helping Britain lead the world in the quest for supersonic flight between the late 1940s and 50s. He was passionate about flying from an early age and was often to be found watching Hawker Fury's with their polished cowlings taking off from his local airfield at Tangmere near Chichester. He enlisted in the RAF in 1938 gaining his 'Wings' in 1939. There was no time for a gentle introduction to the war. As he recalls he was thrown in at the deep end - 'canon fodder' to use his own words describing the thoughts of his instructors, and was stationed with 87 Service Squadron at Lille. This squadron was one of four squadrons operating in France at the time in a futile attempt to stop the German war machine. Here he flew a Hawker Hurricane. The inevitable happened in May 1940 and he was evacuated from France along with the remnants of the squadron and four surviving Hurricanes.

Back in the UK Beamont was sent north to Church Fenton Training Centre in Yorkshire. From here they were sent south to patrol the area over Southampton and Portsmouth as part of 10 Group. Beamont proved himself in the Battle of Britain and was acclaimed an "Ace" with a confirmed tally of five victories. However Beamont is keen to point out in the interview that he gave to Newark Air Museum in August 2000 and to whom I am most grateful for the transcript that they have allowed me to use, he states "each squadron had its own particular brilliant pilots who were already clearly doing a lot better than the rest of us. The rest of us were just doing the best we could, but we weren't encouraged to talk about victories." If a victory was unconfirmed it was logged as "an attack."

It was during this time that Beamont gained valuable experience in night flying. By the end of the Battle of Britain he recounts that pilots had gained enough proficiency in night flying as to not kill themselves in doing so. However he states that the benefit of night flying to Britain at the time was "a waste of time" – searching for a black plane in cloud without radar was near impossible. However the experience was to inspire him for planning future combat tactics. With Britain safe-guarded for the time being after the victory in The Battle of Britain, tactics switched from defensive to offensive. One such being the experimentation of night attacks over enemy territory. Beamont was one of the pilots who flew in Hawker Hurricanes in pairs across the Channel to the Cherbourg Peninsular under the cover of darkness and successfully carried out "investigative ground attacks". Interspersed with long tours of operational duties, pilots were given periods of "so-called" rest which normally meant transfer to Training Command. Beamont opted as his period of 'rest' a post as a Test Pilot for Hawker Aircraft. Hawker by this time was manufacturing and delivering two hundred and fifty aircraft a month each of which had to undergo at least three test flights to check all were air worthy. This was not all plain sailing as Beamont recalls that the normal practice of pilots was "when in trouble – bale out" however as a Test pilot it was the reverse "when in trouble – bring it back!".

During this time Hawker were in the process of developing a far superior fighter – more power, greater speed but design and engine faults led Beamont to declare (despite his genuine fondness for the plane) that the latest offering from Hawker - The Typhoon was "just a bag of nails in bad development trouble – the engines were stopping, tails falling off". However despite this he believed that the Typhoon was a truly great performer and requested on his return to 'ops' that he be given a Typhoon Squadron and so he was - 609 Squadron – West Riding Auxillary.

By now he was a Flight Commander and was leading night and low-level attacks over enemy territory. In September 1942 Hawker unveiled the prototype model of a yet more powerful fighter called the Hawker Tempest. Beamont was the 'Project Pilot' for this "great aeroplane". The Head of 11 Group Air Officer Hugh Sanders asked Beamont to set up the first Tempest wing which was to be based within reach of Normandy and the Pas-de-Calais and operational by April 1944. The Wing comprised of 3, 56, 486 and 150 (of which he was the leader) Squadrons. The Wings role was to play an important part in supporting the Normandy Landings of June 1944. After the success of Normandy the Wing had to focus its attention on another serious threat – the V1 – and destroy it. As it proved, the Tempest was more than capable of the task. Beamont recounts his first sightings of the V1's entering British airspace:

"On 16th June we were called to readiness at dawn with the sky full of things that looked like erratic motorbikes tearing across the sky with streaks of red fire behind them – these were the V1 rockets and at five in the morning Bob Cole, my number two and I, intercepted the first one in daylight off Folkestone and shot it down near Ashford...the Tempest proved extremely successful against flying bombs. At Newchurch, our airfield at Dungeness, we shot down our first hundred in less than two weeks, our first two hundred in three weeks and five hundred in

four and a half weeks. By the end of the V1 campaign, it was very hot that summer, the fighter's had shot down over seven hundred flying bombs of which my wing of Tempests, with three Squadrons, had shot down 638".

Beamont is credited with shooting down thirty-one V1's in the summer of 1944.

With the threat of the V weapons diminished and the Germans on the defensive but fighting harder than ever as the Allies closed in on their frontiers Beamont was moved to the Second Tactical Air Force which was a mere 11 miles from the German border. He recalls a punctual daily shelling was something one got used to at the airfield. Their directive was to maintain air superiority and this meant air-to-air combat as well as ground attack. One of the Squadron's orders was to attack airbases around Hanover which they suspected the Luftwaffe was using as bases for one of their fastest and latest fighters the ME262. Whilst on a sortie to do exactly that Beamont recalls that he spotted an old adversary – a train carrying troops and re-enforcements that he suspected were on route for Arnhem. He believes his suspicions were confirmed by the 'flak mountings' on the train. As he approached for his attack the flak opened up. "Something hit my radiator". Whatever it was forced him to land and he was taken prisoner. Beamont ended up at the infamous Stalag Luft Three POW camp where escape attempts were now forbidden, not on account of the two notorious ones from that camp in 1943 as recounted in the 'The Great Escape' by Paul Brickhill and the second in 'The Wooden Horse' by Eric Williams both former POW's at this camp during these attempts, but, because it was now generally accepted by all sides that Germany's defeat was imminent.

Although peace now ruled in Europe on his repatriation to Britain, war still raged in the Far East and he was asked to form a second Tempest Wing in readiness for combat duty in Burma. During this time he did some test flying of captured German aircraft for Central Fighter Establishment at Tangmere – an experience that he found "most interesting". Wing II was never sent to the Far East as the Japanese surrendered Burma on September 13th 1945. Beamont led the Tempest Wing at the first Battle of Britain flypast in London on 15th September 1945. In January 1946 he was put on the reserve list of the RAF.

After the war Beamont's flying experience and undoubted skill, bravery and love of speed was ideally suited to him continuing with his career as a test pilot. Aircraft were getting faster all the time and following his decision to go on the RAF reserve list he worked for Gloster Aircraft where he was Senior Project Test pilot on the Meteor IV development which was trying to better the RAF's air speed record that they already held. The Meteor was achieving speeds that are technically called 'transonic'. This is when the speed of the aircraft is roughly the equivalent to the speed of sound, but without new designs to cope with this, the aircraft at these speeds were a danger to the pilots. I have an inkling of this unnerving experience when I take my beaten-up Citröen Xantia above the 100km/h mark and the whole body starts to shake! During this period Beamont spent an immensely enjoyable but short period with de Havilland who were building the Vampire. Here he flew around four hundred and fifty of them. In the few years following the war Britain led the way in the development of the jet. The RAF decided that it needed at least six new types of aircraft to keep it at the cutting edge of aviation evolution. Two types of jet fighter were to be developed and four types of jet bomber. In addition they wanted a replacement for the highly successful Mosquito. English Electric was given the project for designing this replacement. Beamont was appointed to lead this project. English Electric had the experience and right engineering partnerships to really pull this off with aplomb. The project was not without its critics though. This was new technology, a new plane design and a new generation of engine 'The Avon Series' from that most revered of companies – Rolls-Royce. The Canberra's prototype test flight passed like a dream "It flew as if it had been flying for a hundred hours – it came off the ground at exactly the predicted speed with exactly the predicted stick forces (as the author is a complete layman he can only explain this is something to do with airspeed and altitude), it was controllable with the fingertips, no muscle force, and right from the first take-off it was a delightful experience." The Canberra took the aviation world by storm. Beamont devised a highly effective air display which astounded the crowd and world press at the Farnborough 1949 Air Show. It was a display that has been described as "like no other has been demonstrated before or is ever likely to be demonstrated again." The display demonstrated how this plane which was categorized as a bomber could out-class many fighters of the day. Interest and orders flooded in from around the world including the USAF. This was the first export of its kind to the States since the DH4 biplane of 1919. The Canberra stayed in service with the RAF for 57 years. It was retired from service on the 23rd June 1969. Beamont and the Canberra set the first transatlantic 'aller-retour' record in 1952 completing the round trip from Northern Ireland to Newfoundland and back (around 2170 miles) in 10 hours 3 minutes. Elizabeth II sent him a congratulatory telegram on his return which he recalled "was a nice way to finish off the day".

Following the success of the Canberra Beamont was test pilot and directly involved in another English Electric success story - the acclaimed supersonic Lightning Fighter in which he regularly achieved Mach 2. In his own words he describes this period in his life as "absolutely splendid". However, winds of change were wafting through the corridors of Whitehall and in 1957 British aviation (and the Military overall) was victim to a huge shake-up. The then Minister of Defence, Duncan Sandys, put forward in a white paper that the future of British Defence interests would not lie in supersonic flight but with missiles. This resulted in huge changes to the structure of the aircraft manufacturing industry. Engine manufacturers Armstrong Siddeley and Bristol's engine division were first to merge in 1959 only to be swallowed up in 1966 by Rolls-Royce. Aside a handful of independent aircraft manufacturers such as Handley Page, Boulton Paul and Scottish Aviation only two big players were left. English Electric, Bristol Aeroplane Company, Vickers Armstrong and Hunting Aircraft were merged to form British Aircraft Corporation (BAC) and de Havilland, Blackburn Aircraft and Folland were merged into Hawker Siddeley who had already converged with Armstrong Whitworth, Avro, Gloster Aircraft and Hawker in 1935. Under new colours in the form of BAC Beamont led the team in developing one of the most advanced supersonic aeroplanes at the time - the TSR2 (Tactical Strike Reconnaissance) aircraft. This was Britain's latest concept of the future in military aviation. Two year's of work had been sweated out, immense brains stretched as well as an investment of thousands of pounds. What was produced has subsequently been described as 'state of the art' and was in some ways ahead of the Tornado that the RAF first flew fifteen years later in 1979. However in 1965 the project was suddenly scrapped along with the aeroplanes that had already been built. This was a bitter blow to Beamont and one of the most unpleasant aspects of the scrapping was that he as a Director of the Board at Warton which was part of BAC now had to "fire many loyal, capable and brilliant engineers".

Beamont now spent much of his time exporting one of the more triumphant stories of the age, namely the Lightning, to Saudi Arabia with great success. For a few decades Beamont recalls that "it was the biggest-earning export programme ever." Beamont remained at BAC until retired in 1979. He continued to fly during his retirement World War One airplanes belonging to the Shuttleworth Collection which he remembered with great affection "I did enjoy that, they were lovely flights". Not wanting to rest easy in his retirement Beamont pursued a literary career in which he succeeded in becoming an aviation author of considerable note. He was presented with many awards throughout his life including an OBE in 1954 and CBE in 1965. He died in 2001. Beamont was posthumously awarded Belgium's highest medal the 'Croix de Guerre' in 2003.

Captain Jean Maridor

The third pilot is Frenchman Captain Jean Maridor. He joined the RAF after the fall of France and flew a Spitfire FXIV in 91 Squadron. A squadron specially designated with the task of intercepting the V1.

At the time of his death Maridor was 23 years old and engaged to be married in August of that year (1944). His story is typical of the bravery and self sacrifice of many young airmen. His story goes that on Thursday 3rd August 1944 at 12.30pm Maridor intercepted a V1 entering British airspace near Rye. He opened up the throttle of his Merlin engine to give chase. Aligning his sights with the target he put in a couple of bursts. Unfortunately these were unsuccessful. Realising that the V1 was now on course to explode in the village of Benenden he opened the throttle to its maximum. The revs of the engine pushed dangerously into the red. Below them lay the peaceful village with its school which was being used as a Red Cross hospital. A red cross was clearly visible on its roof. With no regard for his safety or preservation of his young life Maridor came within fifty metres of the V1. There was little chance of missing this time as his thumb pressed down hard on the fire button. Unleashing a hail of bullets from his four 7.7mm machine guns the V1 exploded under the impact. The remaining fuel and warhead of the flying bomb detonated instantly tearing Maridor's Spitfire apart including ripping off one of the wings. Encased in the doomed and twisted fuselage Maridor plunged to his death and was found close to the school amongst what was left of his aircraft.

The folk of Benenden have never forgotten Maridor's ultimate sacrifice and a permanent memorial has been erected to him in the Village to preserve his memory.

Following hard on the heels of the V1 was the V2. Designed, engineered and project managed by General Walter Dornberger and Dr Wernher von Braun. The V2 had been in the development stages since 1930. Also perfected at Peenemunde the V2 was the world's first Ballistic missile. Requiring cutting edge technology both in shape, warhead and fuel (ethanol and liquid oxygen) much debate was given over to the subject of where and how to launch these monsters.

The matter was passed into the hands of Albert Speer who took over from Dr Todt as Head of the TODT Organisation on his sudden death in 1942. His brief was to build the Atlantic Wall and also the Blockhaus at Eperlecques as it was decided that the best launch method would be from purpose built underground re-enforced concrete bunkers. They were looking for a site that was well connected in terms of transport, closeness to water, naturally camouflaged, near a railway network, close to a supply of electricity and within range of their targets namely London and Antwerp. The forest of Eperlecques near Saint-Omer provided an ideal solution.

Construction started in March 1943. As acres of forest were cleared and considerable building activity was reported back to the Allies the squadrons attached to Operation Crossbow started planning concentrated bombing sorties. Thousands upon thousands of tons of cement, water, sand, crushed stones and reinforcing steel rods would have made their way to the site by barge and lorry.

Between March and August 1943 the 3000 strong workforce needed was largely made up of foreign detainees, notably from the horrific Dora camp in central Germany, in unimaginable conditions. The detainees arrived in sealed cattle trucks near to the heart of the construction site. They were divided into groups of ten with armed guards and work was carried out in 12 hour shifts. The sheer size of the Blockhaus as it exists today is immense and it wouldn't be out of place to say 'overwhelming'. There is nothing good here. What Churchill termed as the 'Wizard War' is easily understandable when one considers the hi-tech scientific research that went into the creation of something designed purely to kill and destroy. The Blockhaus is 22 metres high and covers an area of around 2.5 acres. The Blockhaus was planned initially to be the launch pad for the V2 but after subsequent heavy raids it was decided that its best use would be as the manufacturing plant for the V2 fuel – the highly combustible mixture of ethanol and liquid oxygen.

Five months into the construction Operation Crossbow dropped its first pay-load of bombs. On Friday 27th August 1943 one hundred and eighty five B17's dropped one thousand tons of bombs.

Protecting the bombers were the usual fighter squadrons. One of these squadrons on this occasion was 341 Squadron known as "Alsace". Its leader was a highly capable and experienced fighter pilot named Commandant René Mouchotte. Born in 1914 he went on to become the first Frenchman to command an RAF Squadron. His story is interesting and worthy of inclusion. You will see two plaques dedicated to him at the Blockhaus Eperlecques. Mouchotte despite a strong desire from an early age to become a "Chasseur" or Fighter pilot was instead selected as a Pilot Trainer at the Avord Training Centre at Oran in central France (Department 18). At the signing of the armistice between France and Germany on the 22nd June 1940 he decided with his friend Charles Guérin and some of his co-pilots to flee to Britain. So on the 30th June against express orders not to, they 'borrowed' two planes and flew to Gibraltar. Then hitching a lift on board the armed French Patrol Vessel 'President Houduce' they arrived in Liverpool ten days later – along with many other of their compatriots both service and civilian. Mouchotte was in London on the 14th July 1940 to witness the first review presided over by Général De Gaulle. Mouchotte was then sent to Old Sarum near Salisbury and then to 6 Operational Training Unit at Sutton Bridge. At this time he was training on the Hawker Hurricane. In October 1940 he joined 615 Squadron based at Northolt in London, 615 was then moved to Kenley, south of London. On the 11th October he took part in his first operational sortie. On 4th March he was made a temporary commander of a flight and the following July he was promoted to Flight Commander. On the 26th August he claimed his first victory – a Junkers 88.

On 10th November 1941 he was transferred to the RAF Turnhouse in Scotland. Here he joined 340 Squadron which had only been formed three days earlier. This was the Free French fighter arm of the RAF known as the 'Ile de France' equipped with Spitfires. Their initial duty was to conduct defensive patrols over the skies of southern Scotland and the North Sea. In February 1942 No 2 Group of which 340 was a part, was placed under the command of Philippe de Scitivaux which meant that Mouchotte replaced him as Head of 'A' Flight or "Paris" as it was known. A month later Mouchotte was promoted to Flight Lieutenant.

In January 1943 Mouchotte took command of 341 Squadron whose motto was "Friendship". The Squadron had previously taken part in sorties over the Western Dessert and on its return to the UK was based briefly at RAF Turnhouse before moving to Biggin Hill south London in March 1943 to start operational sweeps over France. The 'sector' in which 341 Squadron operated was by 15th May 1943 fast approaching a milestone of one thousand victories over the Luftwaffe. A sweepstake was organised between the squadrons and there was much excitement as to who would claim the £185 prize for the 1000th victory. 341 "Alsace" Squadron took off on the 15th May on a protection sortie over France. When over the Pas-de-Calais the attacking force was set upon by a large pack of Focke Wolfe 190's. During fierce dogfights Squadron Leader EFJ Charles and Mouchotte both claimed the 999th and 1000th kill but no-one was sure whose was downed first or second so it was mutely accepted that the cash prize be shared between the two pilots.

Mouchotte's final sortie occurred on August 27th 1943 when the squadron flew a protection sortie to bomb the Blockhaus d'Eperlecques. By this date it was his 342nd war sortie and as his diary states his *"fatigue is merciless and I can feel my nerves breaking. I have an unbearable need for rest. I haven't taken a week's leave in over two years. Always on the alert to fly. I am worn out..."* Whatever happened no-one was quite sure suffice to say that he never returned and was posted missing. His body was washed up on a Belgian beach near the town of Middlekerke on September 3rd 1943 where he was buried. His body was exhumed in October 1949 and laid to rest in the family vault at Père-Lachaise Cemetery in Paris in November of the same year. He was awarded the Croix de la Libération by de Gaulle in July 1942 and the Distinguished Flying Cross in September 1942 for "acts of gallantry when flying in active operations against the enemy".

Within eleven days after Mouchotte's disappearance a mélange of B25's, Marauders, Venturas, Mosquitos, Halifaxs, Wellingtons and B17s dropped over 2100 bombs on the Blochhaus and construction was halted. The Nazis were forced to reconsider. Only temporarily however. An engineer called Floss came up with a solution. He proposed that a five metre thick concrete 'umbrella' be placed over the construction site. This shield became known as 'the tortoise'. Construction would continue from the base up and as the bunker grew in height enormous hydraulic jacks would raise the roof accordingly. The idea was approved; new forced labour victims were drafted in, construction continued and then came more bombing.

From February to August 1944 an assortment of 862 bombers dropped in the region of 4619 bombs. Evidence of this is all around you with the pock-marked forest floor. This payload of explosive does not including thirty-two 'Tallboy' bombs. These immense earth tremblers were developed by Barnes Wallis of 'Bouncing Bomb' fame. Specially adapted Avro Lancasters were the only aircraft able to carry them as the bombs themselves weighed in at around 5.5 tons and were over 6 metres long. They were used against the Blockhaus on two occasions the first being Monday 19th June 1944 when seventeen were dropped. One landed forty-six metres from the Blockhaus creating an enormous crater literally shaking its foundations, then on Tuesday 25th July 1944 fifteen more were dropped.

Bombing raids continued on Friday 25th August by a force of Halifax, Lancaster and Mosquito aircraft dropping 1000 and 2000 lb bombs. The Blockhaus was abandoned after that without a V2 ever launched from it. Today this once secretive and sinister area is a worthwhile museum open most of the year offering guided tours as well as individual visits.

The vast concrete dome that is its namesake still looms large on the slopes near Wizernes

© *La Coupole*

After the 'disablement' of the Blockhaus at Eperlecques work began on what can only be described as one of the most ambitious engineering projects undertaken on behalf of Hitler's Nazi regime. Like Eperlecques this vast concrete structure was designed to house and launch the V2 stratospheric rocket. Similar to the Blockhaus at Eperlecques it became a matter of top priority to ensure its destruction and thus it became a key target for airmen attached to the bomber squadrons of the RAF and USAF in Operation Crossbow.

Construction began on La Coupole (Dome) in October 1943. Today it is not beyond the realms of our imaginations to get to grips with the horror and human suffering that went into the construction of the building. The main entrance Tunnel which still serves as the main access point to the interior is cavernous, cold and eerily hair-raising. As you proceed further into the interior the damp clammy air begins to cling to you, the lights flicker to the accompaniment of exploding bombs and the relentless undertone of hammering and hacking at the rock walls by its wretched labourers. La

Coupole required a daily workforce of one thousand three hundred people. Sixty percent were Foremen or Qualified German Personnel the remainder was made up of French men forced to work under the terms of the Service du Travail Obligatoire (STO Compulsory Work Service) - and Soviet prisoners of war which included many women. The working conditions like any building project under the Todt organisation were horrific: brutal, harsh, merciless and relentless. Building continued under a seven day round the clock building programme. The Germans had seen the advantages of a protective cover as in their tortoise shell at Eperlecques but here at la Coupole they wanted to ensure impenetrable protection.

So, in January 1944 work started on creating a single concrete piece dome weighing a colossal 55 000 tonnes. Regular sorties to destroy this building started in March 1944. The dome at this point in time was complete and proved its indestructibility in withstanding sixteen major bombing sorties against it which dropped in the region of three thousand tonnes of bombs. The dome remained intact despite extensive damage around the site. Unsurprisingly the town of Wizernes was very badly damaged. Two raids did however put pay to the significant threat that La Coupole presented to the civilised world. On Monday 24th June and Monday 17th July 1944 RAF Lancasters from the infamous 617 Squadron of "Dambuster" fame managed to successfully drop a number of 'Tall Boy' bombs. The latter raid caused irreparable damage in managing to shift the Dome out of alignment and also causing the collapse of the chalk cliff from which the vast structure is hewn blocking the entrance tunnels.

Hitler's dream of being able to liberally bombard London at will from La Coupole never materialised - not a single V2 was launched from here either. It is horribly ironic that the cost in human life lost lay in the construction of the two concrete bunkers near Saint-Omer and building the rockets themselves rather than in the number that fell victim to their detonation.

Hitler ordered the project of building La Coupole be abandoned on Friday 28th July 1944. The V2 project was not abandoned however. There was very little anyone could do about them. They were too fast to intercept and their mobile launchers were difficult to search out but fortunately the war was already lost for Nazi Germany. Three thousand V2 rockets were launched killing 8 938 people in England and 6 500 people in Belgium. After the fall of France it was the British Secret Service that was given the task of 'liberating' La Coupole. They sealed the tunnel by 'blowing' huge charges of explosive, leaving the horror to be unearthed decades later.

The Blockhaus d'Eperlecques and La Coupole are today two of the most important museums in France. Having been abandoned for decades they have only relatively recently become major historic attractions of the area and are rightly Historic Monuments to a period that is still very fresh in people's minds. The two musems have many links and joint exhibitions with UK establishments such as the Imperial War Museum in London. In 2012 La Coupole opened an impressive Planetarium.

Group Captain Sir Douglas Robert Steuart Bader CBE, DSO, DFC, FRAeS, DL
by Paul Ferdinand Anton Laib, © National Portrait Gallery, London

Before recounting this fascinating tale I thought, just in case there is any reader uncertain of whom this flying legend was, a quick potted account of his life is necessary. Douglas Robert Steuart Bader was born on Monday 21st February 1910 in St John's Wood in London. Not particularly keen on his studies yet still obtaining offers of places from both Oxford and Cambridge Universities Bader preferred to concentrate on his sporting endeavours namely Cricket and Football. Whilst at St Edwards School in Oxford his then headmaster, Reverend Henry Kendall strongly urged him to consider taking up a Cadetship at RAF Cranwell. Bader took this on board and found flying came naturally to him making his first solo flight after just 11 hours 15 minutes having completed the training with his instructor, Flying Officer W J "Pissy" Pearson. Flying Officer Pearson was apparently strict in not allowing Americanisms to describe his aircraft - it was an aeroplane and not a 'kite' etc.

Now a Pilot Officer, Bader continued to excel not only in the air but on the playing field. He played fly half for Harlequins and batted for the RAF First XI Cricket Team. Life was exciting and full of promise for the 21 year old Bader when tragedy struck on Monday 14th December 1931 at the Reading Aero Club. Bader crashed his Bulldog Mark IIa whilst doing some low level aerobatics. In his diary recollections he recalls "Crashed slow-rolling near ground. Bad show". For the athletic Bader this was an extreme understatement. However losing what amounted to a third of his body was to make him one of the most famous pilots of all time and one of the human race's most impressively determined examples.

Bader spent the next couple of years recovering, learning to walk with his prosthetic legs, drive, play golf, learn to fly and even dance. He managed also to find the time to marry Thelma Edwards on Thursday 5th October 1933. Despite the huge amount achieved the RAF revoked its approval for his fitness for active service because his case was not covered in the Kings regulations. He was invalided out of the RAF in May 1933.

At the outbreak the Second World War Bader left his then employer, The Asiatic Petroleum Company and after initial difficulties was accepted as being fit for active service. Bader joined 19 Squadron in February 1939 based at RAF Duxford. He discovered soon after that he had distinct advantage over his fellow pilots which was that, being legless his blood could not flow to his legs thus warding off a side effect of 'G' force – namely passing out.

In April 1940 he joined 222 Squadron as a Flight Commander. Here he scored up his first couple of victories. In June 1940 he was promoted to Squadron Leader and moved to 242 Squadron. The Battle of Britain had by now begun and Bader won recognition not only as a formidable Pilot but also in his support of using the 'Big Wing' – which meant attacking the Luftwaffe en masse using three to five squadrons of aircraft at a time.

In 1941 he was promoted to Wing Commander and stationed at RAF Tangmeer in West Sussex flying Spitfires. By August 1941 Bader had claimed 22.5 victories and was one of the highest scoring pilots of the RAF at that time.

After Bader was forced to bale out of his Spitfire in August 1941 he was treated in Saint-Omer for an injury sustained to his shoulder and also took possession of a right replacement leg dropped by the RAF in what they termed as 'Leg Operation'. In true character Bader became somewhat of an escape artist and eventually found himself installed in the escape-proof neo classic style fortress of Colditz Castle. Here he remained until the end of the war when he was liberated by US 1st Army on Sunday 15th April 1945.

After the war Bader remained in the RAF until February 1946 where upon he took up a job with Royal Dutch Shell. Bader championed the cause of disabled people, an undertaking that was officially recognised by a knighthood bestowed upon him in 1976. He died from a heart attack following an official dinner given in honour of the 90th Birthday of Sir Arthur 'Bomber' Harris on the 4th September 1982. Countless projects, buildings, awards and incentive schemes have been set up using his name, and Saint-Omer is no different as can be seen in rue du Soleil in which stands Résidence D. Bader, but the greatest of these has to be the charitable trust set up by his friends and fellow pilots after his death: The Douglas Bader Foundation.

The first association made by the Bader family with Saint-Omer was during the First World War by his father Frederick Roberts Bader, who was buried somewhere in Saint-Omer in 1921 after sustaining a horrific shrapnel injury in World War One. The whereabouts of his grave is unknown.

The second association started on Friday 8th August 1941 when the invincible Squadron Leader Douglas Bader ran out of luck and was forced to bale out of his doomed Spitfire Mark VA over the Pas-de-Calais after his tail was spliced off due to either friendly fire or a mid-air collision.

He wounded his shoulder and lost his right prosthetic leg. He landed in a field close to the village of Boeseghem near Aire-sur-la-Lys (35) where he was taken into captivity by three German soldiers. From Boeseghem he was taken to the German Clinique in Saint-Omer known as Clinique Stérin at 59 rue Saint-Bertin.

Clinique Stérin where Bader was treated, stayed at and escaped from in rue St-Bertin

© *Photo Jonathan Caton*

The following details his attempted escape from this clinic in August 1941 and has been admirably researched and retold by Raymond Dufay in his book *La Vie dans l'Audomarois Sous l'Occupation.*

It was not the first time that the area around *Clinique Stérin in rue Saint-Bertin* was subject to attempted escapes. Four British soldiers had planned and executed exactly that a year earlier in October 1940.

Our story stars Squadron Leader Bader and four brave Saint-Omerians, Mr and Madame Hiecque (both retired) of *129 quai du Haut-Pont,* Madame Lucile Debacker, 25 years old of *20 boulevard Clémenceau* and employed as a *'Fille de Salle'* at Clinique Stérin and finally Gilbert Petit, 29 years old and living at *130 quai du Haut-Pont.* All three and their families were fervently patriotic to France.

Anti-German sentiment had been running high in Saint-Omer. Only a few weeks before on Bastille Day an impromptu 'promenade' had taken place whereby all participants had worn badges of solidarity and dressed where possible in colours resembling the '*Tricolores*'. A French flag had also been erected on a pylon near to the lock of the *Quatre-Moulins* with a notice defying any French National to dare take it down: "*Malheur au Francais qui enlèvera ce drapeau.*"

Bader was famous and known to the Luftwaffe and his capture would have been 'news' that rippled through the town. It soon became known that the inexhaustible Bader was looking to escape. His intentions came to the attention of Madame Debacker who passed the information to Mr and Mrs Hiecque. Being retired, the two were unsure that they would be able to help but thought their neighbour Mr Petit might be able to assist Bader. This was indeed the case.

Considerable detail has been discovered concerning Bader's accommodation in rue Saint-Bertin at the clinic. We know that he was staying in Room 21 on the 2nd floor. His nurses were Mme Lucille Debacker whom we have already met and a Melle Raymonde Wépierre. There was a round the clock guard outside his door. Being a 'prized' and respected prisoner Bader enjoyed – under the circumstances - considerable trappings of luxury. His meals were served on fine porcelain plates. Dufay's source lists that Bader was served bread and butter, orange marmalade, slices of ham, and tea served from a teapot with a cup and saucer and a silver spoon in which to stir in milk served from a little matching jug.

His German attendants found Bader to possess "monstrous cheek" and that he was "hot headed" and a man of exceptional character. One German orderly, a Mr Fritz noted in one of his daily reports that Bader jostled with him on the stairs.

The esteem in which Bader was held is clearly supported by the fact that on his demand for a replacement leg the authorisation came swiftly and direct from the top of the Luftwaffe. Herman Goering no less gave his assurance that safe passage would be granted to the prosthetic that would be parachuted in from Britain by the RAF. The Luftwaffe also played host to him as the acclaimed fighter pilot with artificial legs. The German fighter Ace Adolf 'Dolfo' Galland (whom he befriended after the war) organised a formal tea for Bader at one of the airfields surrounding Saint-Omer. Galland arranged that his prized Horch motorcar accompanied by an officer, an adjutant and chauffeur pick him up to bring him to the party. Bader was visibly surprised by the warm reception and in the clever way in which the aerodrome had been disguised. A long discussion then took place regarding the technicalities of the visual deceptions. Galland recounts in his book '*The First and the Last*' that Bader with typical gall asked him if he would do him a favour? To which Galland replied "*If I am able it will be a pleasure*", to which Bader replied "*I'd like once in my life to fly a Messerschmitt. Let me do a circuit of the aerodrome.*" Bader fixed Galland with a sparkle in his eyes and as Galland recalled later, he nearly weakened to the request.

Lieutenant General Adolf Galland © Stéphane Milamon

Back at the hospital Bader shared a ward with three others. The first was a young man from London called Willie who had been wounded in his palate by a piece of shrapnel, the second was a Pilot from one the RAF Eagle Squadrons called Bill Hall who had a smashed kneecap from a bullet and the third was a Polish pilot who had been badly burned on his face but because he could speak French, acted as interpreter for the small group to their carers Lucile Debacker and Raymonde Wépierre.

Baders' ward was twelve metres above the ground and was guarded in the same fashion as his room in rue Saint-Bertin. The courtyard far below was quiet and unguarded. Willie and the Polish pilot were due for transfer imminently for Germany. Bader did not have a lot of time to wait. He knew that his transfer would soon arrive. He became impatient but was told by Lucile that he would have to wait until Sunday to see if it were possible for him to be helped to escape. It was only Thursday. The few days that he had to wait he passed by pretending to be weaker and more shaken than he really was – in order to delay any possible notion of a transfer to Germany.

Meanwhile Lucile put the escape plan into action by opening the chain of communication between the different French volunteers needed to make the escape possible. She was also responsible for acquiring a sufficient number of sheets that would make safe the twelve metre drop from Bader's bed to freedom. With all the arrangements made she delivered on her lunch round to the patients a scrap of paper to Bader. The escape was to be attempted on Sunday 17th August 1941.

It had already been noticed that during this particular month there had been considerable activity in the air from the RAF. If this continued as was hoped it would provide ideal cover to make his escape. Sunday evening proved impossible, Monday also but Tuesday proved ideal. Mr Petit waited for Bader. Bader made good his escape and shinned down the sheets. He found Mr Petit who attracted him by drawing heavily on a cigarette three times. Bader approached the Frenchman. *"Can I trust you"* he asked. *"Yes, follow me."*

Mr Petit gave Bader an overcoat and a hat as disguise and off they set. Bader did not find the route easy. In fact - anything but. His stumps hurt him and he walked ungainly and noisily through the blacked out streets of Saint-Omer. Gilbert Petit stuck to the smaller roads taking the following route. Together they crossed the wide cobbled street of *rue Saint-Bertin* and continued on their way as quickly as possible up *rue du Tambour* towards *Place St Jean*. Here they passed the *Salle de Concert*.

Street sign for rue du Tambour the first leg of Bader's journey © Photo Jonathan Caton

The cobbles in this large square were not helping the chaffing of Bader's stumps. Still sticking to the side streets Mr Petit and Bader continued down *rue de l'Oeil*, and crossed the wide street of *rue Carnot* undetected. Here they continued their dangerous journey down *rue Guillaume Cliton*. From *rue Guillaume Cliton* they crossed another normally busy street, *rue de Dunkerque* and into *rue Hendricq*.

At the end of *rue Hendricq* Bader and Mr Petit turned down *rue du Soleil* (passing what is now known as Résidence Bader) – still undetected but Bader was in considerable discomfort by this stage.

Tired but still undetected Bader and Petit continued on their escape path down rue du Soleil
©*Photo Jonathan Caton*

All went well until they arrived at the *Boulevard de Strasbourg*. Here, a German patrol forced Bader to hide in the entrance way of the Brasserie Guilbert, *61 Boulevard de Strasbourg*. Mr Petit continued acknowledging the patrol as he passed them. Once they had passed and the coast was clear he went back to collect the Wing Commander.

Despite his determination and high pain threshold Bader was now finding that his right stump in particular was causing him great discomfort. There was still a considerable way to go before they reached safety. At this point at the entrance to the Haut-Pont Gilbert hoisted Bader onto his back and carried him the rest of the way to *129 Quai du Haut Pont*: The home of Mr and Mme Hiecque. Gilbert Petit did not stay long. He wanted to get home, recover and get some sleep as he started work at 05h00 at the train station.

Bader meanwhile stayed in the Hiecque's house and by all accounts was completely spent and slept soundly. In the early morning Mme Petit arrived at the house and helped soothe Bader's enflamed stumps. She bathed them and redressed them using fleece and tights.

Meanwhile up at the hospital Bader's escape was discovered and all hell was let loose. All the staff were questioned and under some considerable duress one of them 'cracked'. Revealing Bader's probable whereabouts - 129 rue Haut Pont. The Germans did not waste time making their way to the Haut Pont.

On hearing the commotion outside their house Mr Hiecque hurried Bader into the garden to hide in a small shed at the back of the garden. Inside he saw garden implements stacked against the walls and a large pile of straw. Bader 'dived' into the straw burying himself. This was not to be a routine search as the Germans had had the tip off. Their escapee was here along with his assailants. They were not going to fail in their quest to find him. Arriving at the shed and entering, it was not long before Bader was rooted out. Particularly as he recounted that a bayonet had passed a couple of inches from his nose and another had gone through the sleeve of his jacket. Bader gave himself up and was quickly escorted from the premises. On passing Mr Hiecque, Bader insisted to his German captors that they knew nothing of his presence. It was about 08h15.

The Germans arrested Mr Petit, Mr and Mrs Hiecque - though Madame was not in her house at the time of Bader's arrest, she had left the house to go and get her radio repaired - and Lucile Debacker. The four were imprisoned and interrogated. On Tuesday 9th September 1941 Lucile Debacker and the retired couple Mr and Mrs Hiecque were sentenced to death by a military tribunal. Newspaper headlines for the 10th September printed the headline "Condemned for helping a British Pilot escape". Mr Petit escaped charge on account that his comrades did not break under interrogation and there was no proof that it was he who had aided Bader.

By a most fortunate official intervention on behalf of the accused the three had their death sentences quashed. Instead their sentences were changed and they were deported to the horrific labour camps. Mr Hiecque was sent to Diez Lahn and Mme Hiecque and Lucile Debacker to Anrath bei Kreifeld. Miraculously the three survived their ordeal and after the war they returned to Saint-Omer. Mr Hiecque died in 1952 and Gilbert Petit in 1963. It is not the end of the story however.

Bader returned to Saint-Omer on the 8th May 1965 as a guest of honour to witness the presentation of the 'Croix Légion d'Honneur' to the sole survivor of this extraordinary story - Mme Maria Hiecque. As for Bader? He was made an honourable citizen of Saint-Omer.

Happier times. Bader with the only surviving escape 'coup de main' Madame Maria Hiecque marking her bravery with the presentation of the 'Croix Légion d'Honneur'
8th May 1965 © L'Indépendant

Liberation Day for Saint-Omer Tuesday 5th September 1944

Relief and an end to occupation came to Saint-Omer when General Maczek of the Polish Army led the 1st Tank Corps into Saint-Omer on Tuesday 5th September 1944 at around 16h30 via *rue d'Arras* and liberated the town.

The Polish Memorial in rue d'Arras ©Photo Jonathan Caton

Liberation! Place Foch 5th September 1944 © Association Devoir de Mémoire

The fighting stubbornly continued right up until the last moment. The FFI *"Forces Françaises de l'Intérieur"* and the CDLR *"Ceux de la Résistance"* (Lit: Those from the Resistance) played a major part in flushing out the Germans from the town before the Poles arrived to the sight of a French Flag flying defiantly from the recently vacated German Headquarters in *Place Victor Hugo*. In the *Place Foch* you will see on the wall of the Banque de France building two plaques commemorating the death of the same person: Albert Minet. The reason why there are two plaques is because they are representative of two different French resistance groups: The FFI and CDLR. Other plaques in the town for the same day are seen in rue Louis Martel commemorating the loss of life of Emile Cantré in *rue Jacqueline Robins* for Lucien Leroy FFI and CDLR and in Boulevard de Strasbourg for a Polish soldier and another Resistance member André Bultel. Following hard on the caterpillar tracks of the Poles as liberators were the Canadians. The French of today never forget their sacrifice and flowers are placed each year on September 5th by The Mairie below each plaque.

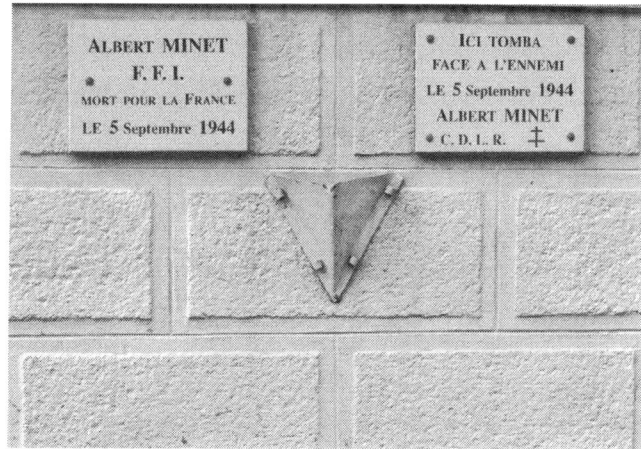

Memorial plaques to Albert Minet (Grand Place), André Bultel and Jacob Galusinski (Boulevard de Strasbourg). Photos Jonathan Caton

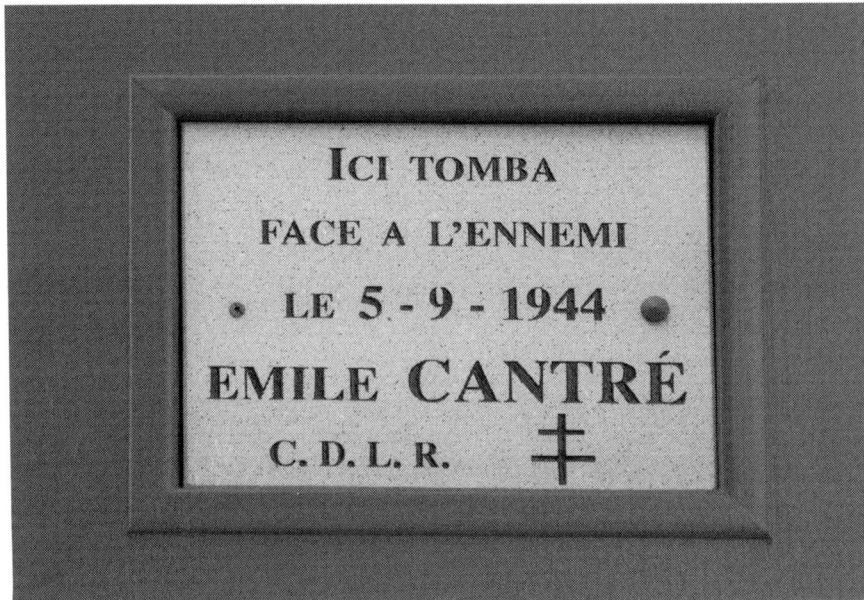

Plaques dedicated to Emile Cantré (rue Louis Martel) and Lucien Leroy
(rue Jacqueline Robins) Photos Jonathan Caton

During my many visits to the Souvenir Cemetery researching for this book I noticed that amongst the hundreds of servicemen there from the Army in particular there are the graves of six sailors, two of these "unknown". I was curious to find out more because Saint-Omer is some distance from the sea and in some cases miles from the location of the wrecks.

The first sailor is Able Seaman William George Barlow RN serving on merchantman SS Dungrange. She was torpedoed and sunk on 19th June 1944 on route for the Normandy beaches with a cargo of ammunition. She was sunk by a German E boat, 25 miles from the Normandy beaches.

The second is Chief Engine Room Artificier Horace James Millard RN serving on HMS Keith. HMS Keith was a Class B Destroyer launched in 1930. She was sunk off the coast of Belgium (adjacent to De Panne), on Saturday 1st June 1940 whilst trying to evacuate troops from the beaches in Operation Dynamo. She was attacked by Luftwaffe Stukas and after her boiler room took a direct hit the order was given to abandon ship. 36

sailors died in the attack but 130 escaped. However of this total 100 were lost later that day when their rescue tug HMS Saint Abbs was sunk due to further air attacks.

The third sailor was onboard the mine sweeper HMS Skipjack at the evacuation of troops from Dunkerque. His name is Able Seaman Alfred Thomas Chitral Hammond. He was among the nineteen crew and 275 troops that died that day. On Saturday 1st June 1940 at 08h00 HMS Skipjack was circling at full speed in an attempt to avoid being hit by a massive aerial attack. When not circling she was slowing down to pick up fleeing soldiers from the beaches of Dunkerque. By 08h44 HMS Skipjack had rescued 275 terrified and exhausted troops. At 08h45 ten Luftwaffe Ju88's targeted the ship. Within five minutes she had been hit five times. Panic stricken men dived into the icy water only to be machine-gunned. Meanwhile the ship lasted only twenty minutes. She went down with most of her crew and human cargo.

The fourth sailor is from the merchant navy. His name is Frederick Stanley Rowson. He was 'Mate' on board MV Ashanti. He died on Saturday 10th June 1944 when his ship was torpedoed.

The destructive effects of World War Two continued long after the war had finished. In 1947 the Tower of Saint-Bertin collapsed having been weakened a couple of years before by an Allied bomb that had destroyed many of the tower's supporting trajectories.

The final indignity to the ruins of L'Abbaye St-Bertin – 1947
© Société Académique des Antiquaires de la Morinie

Saint-Omer's association with the British Army and the Royal Air Force continues. The Army named one of their barracks, St-Omer in Aldershot, after the town and the RAF continue to attend Armistice Day ceremonies both in the town and at the aerodrome.

In recent times the British Connection has continued thanks to the services of one of the last soldiers from the First World War alive at the time of writing – Henry Allingham. Returning in 2004 for the first time in 85 years to an area that held so many conflicting memories for him, he was made an honorary citizen of the town by a former Mayor of Saint-Omer, Jean-Jacques Delvaux and the citizens of Saint-Omer. Always an ambassador for promoting peace Henry Allingham spent a long time conversing with students from the College de L'Esplanade in Saint-Omer. On this occasion (11th September 2004) he was present as an Honoured Guest to unveil the British Air Services Memorial at the aerodrome and was a regular attendee for the annual 11th November Armistice Services thereafter.

The Ch'Ti Language

Over the passage of time we have seen that l'Audomarois has a very confusing and complex history. This is also true of the local dialect: Ch'Ti or Ch'Timi. Ch'Ti is the local patois and has its own language rules and peculiarities. According to the official UNESCO description of the language it is a variant on the Picard language spoken throughout the north of France and in parts of Belgium. UNESCO has listed the patois as one of the 'endangered' languages on the planet. In a recent study by Jean-Michel Eloy, Professor of Linguistics at the Jules Verne University of Picardy suggests that just 12% of the population where this dialect originates actually speak it. Its origins lie in Latin. It was once the primary language used by miners, farmers and labourers in Picardy, Nord Pas-de-Calais and in some parts of Belgium. The language has had its fair share of 'image problems' with some people recoiling in horror if the language was used to address them!

The language has recently had a boom of publicity throughout France and Europe due to the huge success of a French film starring amongst other notables the French Comedian Dany Boon: "*Bienvenue Chez les Ch'tis*".

It is a charming film telling the story of a Manager of 'La Poste', Phillipe Abrams (Kad Merad) who has to relocate areas for professional reasons from the South of France to Bergues in the Nord-Pas-de-Calais. Needless to say his family and he are appalled at the prospect. Even a 'gendarme' on the Autoroute sympathises with him and lets him off his offence for driving too slowly en route to his Northern destination. However the warmth and generous spirit of this wonderful area prevail and Monsieur Abrams of La Poste is a convert. I am not fluent in French and doubt I ever will be, and so the comedy surrounding the use of the Ch'Ti language was lost on me to a large degree but I enjoyed the film very much all the same.

Educational links with the UK

Saint-Omer continues its historical path as a centre of learning and there are many schools, colleges, lycées and further education establishments in the town. Many of these have strong links with similar institutions in the UK but there is always a constant search for new connections. One partnership that is very strong concerns the *Collège de St-Bertin*.

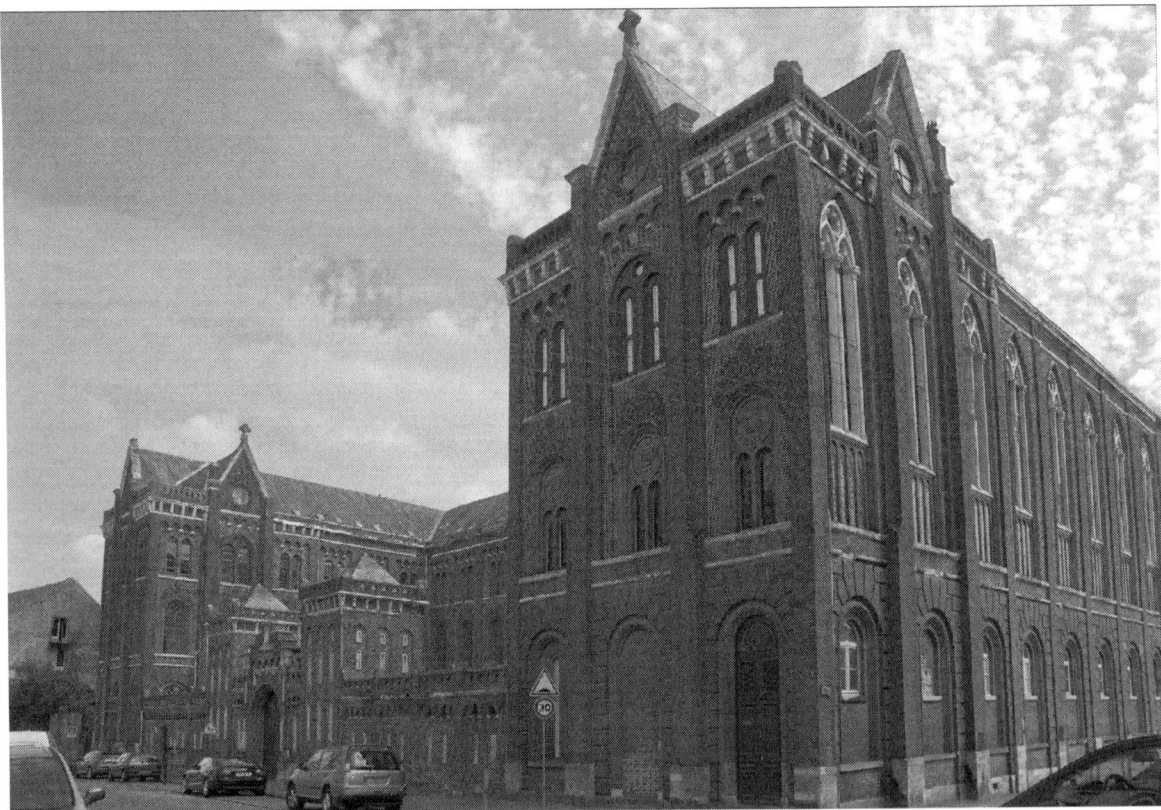

Collège de St-Bertin, rue St-Bertin © Photo Jonathan Caton

This *Collège* was built in 1813 as a successor to the first *Collège St-Bertin* set up by Abbot Gérard d'Haméricourt who as we now know had much to do with establishing the Jesuit community in Saint-Omer in 1567. Built in red brick and in the style known as '*Style Anglaise*'. The layout of this impressive building originally consisted of two rectangular blocks which provided accommodation; teaching and eating areas and a third block which is a Chapel. The three blocks enclose a small gravelled Quad which opens onto *rue St-Bertin*. Inside there remain many original features, one being a magnificent timbered rectangular staircase which carries the weight, wear and tear of hundreds of pupils every day.

The school was run by the Benedictines and was a feeder school for the French Military and also has a strong Musical heritage. Amongst its past alumni is Général Pétain who revisited the school when he met British Prime Minister Asquith in May 1915. The school today is much larger that it was originally and remains a thriving part of Saint-Omer's educational community. It has a long established link and exchange scheme with Dame Alice Owens School in Potters Bar, Hertfordshire.

The future...

Today Saint-Omer relies on tourism, glass manufacture, brewing (as seen in the two pictures below) friendly people and the clear fact it is a very worthwhile place to visit.

The Brasserie L'Audomaroise © Photo Jonathan Caton

Saint-Omer Brasserie © Photo Jonathan Caton

The town has in recent years received funding from both the EU and from various tourism enterprises within France. The town maintains considerable links with the UK through school exchange programmes, twin towning (Deal, Ypres and Detmold in Germany), joint cultural and sporting events but more importantly through its unbreakable links through our shared history.

Bonne Visite, Bonne Route et Bon Retour!

Saint-Omer Coat of Arms © Ville de Saint-Omer

Acknowledgments

I would like to express my sincere thanks to the many people who have helped, organized and encouraged me in my research for the creation of this book. At the outset I would like to thank Jonathan Caton for the many hours and enormous contribution that he gave me and the project through the lens of his camera.

On the French side I would like to thank Le Maire de Saint-Omer Bruno Magnier and his team for the necessary and various authorizations required to carry out aspects of this project. This book would not have been possible save for the great assistance from the following organisations and individuals both locally and elsewhere who have provided me with information, books, photos, waived or reduced fees, leads, money, essential office equipment and encouragement. These people and establishments include the Blockhaus D'Eperlecques, La Coupole, Le Musée de l'hôtel Sandelin and in particular Sarah Vallin (Curator), Dany Clairet (Secretary), the Department Ville d'Art et d'Histoire de Saint-Omer, Philippe Queste (Director), Cécile Albagnac (Deputy), the Société Académique des Antiquaires de la Morinie and in particular Charles Debacker (President), Rose-Marie Pasquier (Secretary and Librarian), Bernard Level (Vice President), Henri Lorge (Treasurer), the members of l'Association Devoir de Mémoire, La Bibliothèque de Saint-Omer particularly the Director Françoise Ducroquet, Archivist Natalie Rébéna and Librarian Olivier Ferlin, l'Indépendant newspaper notably Nöel Devos, La Distillerie de Houlle, local historian Stéphane Milamon, François Mulet and Le Parc Naturel Régional Caps et Marais d'Opale, La Bibliothèque Nationale de France, Historian Paul Barsoum, Mireille Cocquerel, Raymond Karczynski, Alexandre & Christine Kuoch, L'Abbé Pierre Lepetit, Lionel & Moira Le Ven, Ros Levy, David & Pelo Myerscough-Jones, Marie Sammut-Oyer, Nicole Scott, Maurice & Heide Sellier and Mathew Van Dyk.

On the English side I am enormously grateful to The RAF Museum at Hendon, Peter Dye and Peter Daybell, The Imperial War Museum London, The Ministry of Defence, The London Transport Museum, The National Army Museum, Stonyhurst College and in particular David Knight for his help on the section covering St-Omers

College, Maurice Whitehead, Professor of History at Swansea University for his help with finding images and information on the Carroll Family, The Douglas Bader Foundation, Graham Berry for his help with providing information on Joseph Berry, and likewise Howard Heeley and the Newark Air Museum for his help with 'Bee Beamont, Maria Singer and The Yale Center for British Art, Bridget Clifford and the Royal Armories Museum, Robert Solly and The Sole Society, The National Gallery, London, The National Portrait Gallery, London, The V&A Museum London, The Commonwealth War Graves Commission, Steve Rogers and The War Graves Photographic Project, The Royal Collection, Tim Donovan, Alex Sayers and last but by no means least to my sons Xavier and Fabien who gave me added morale at times of need and finally to my wife Gisi who has given me unfailing support, belief and many nights poring over text and to whom this book is sincerely dedicated.

REFERENCES

1   PEARSE: Scenes from the History of Saint-Omer 1917, Lecture to the Munro Institute in Saint-Omer 1917 Imperial War Museum, London

2   Dr D G HESSAYON: The Vegetable & Herb Expert Pg 44 Printed by Expert Books, Transworld Publishers ISBN 0 903505 46 0

3   PEARSE: Scenes from the History of Saint-Omer 1917 – Lecture to the Munro Institute in Saint-Omer 1917 Imperial War Museum, London

4   Walking the Walls – Historic Defences of Saint-Omer and Page 20 of Histoire de Saint-Omer, Lille Press

5   J. M. KEMBLE, The Saxons in England, (London: Quaritch, 1876), Vol. II, Appendix, p.528, reprinted in Roy C. Cave & Herbert H. Coulson, A Source Book for Medieval Economic History, (Milwaukee: The Bruce Publishing Co., 1936; reprint ed., New York: Biblo & Tannen, 1965), pp. 200-202.

6   Frank BARLOW:Thomas Becket, Phoenix Press 2000 ISBN 1 84212 4277 taken from Chapter 7: Thomas on the Defensive November 1164 – April 1166

7   Annuaire 1908 St-Omer et de son arrondissement. Printer : Memorial Artisan pg 75

8   Annuaire 1908 St-Omer et de son arrondissement. Printer : Memorial Artisan pg 75

9   Eileen POWER: The Wool Trade in English Medieval History, Ford Lecture 1941

10   L'arrondissement de Saint-Omer dans le passé et le présent 1924 Pg 42

11   L'arrondissement de Saint-Omer dans le passé et le présent 1924 Pg 59

12   Barbara TUCHMAN: A Distant Mirror – A calamitous 14th Century Page 94 ISBN 0 333197 52 6 1978 printed by Macmillan London Ltd

13   The Burlington Magazine Vol 124 No 949 Pp219

14   Henriette PETERS: Mary Ward: A world in Contemplation Pg 74 translated by Helen Butterworth Printers: Fowler Wright Books 1994 ISBN 0 85244 268 8

15   Hubert CHADWICK: St Omers to Stonyhurst Page 11 Printers Burns Oates 1962

16   Hubert CHADWICK: St Omers to Stonyhurst Pg 84 Printers Burns Oates 1962

17   Hubert CHADWICK: St Omers to Stonyhurst Pg 50 Printers Burns Oates 1962

18 Bernard LEVEL: L'Enclos Saint-Bertin reflet des Difficultés d'une ville Saint-Omer 1780-1947 458th Edition Tome: XIV Jan 2001 for Les Antiquaires de la Morinie

19 Bernard LEVEL: Le Futur Admiral Nelson à Saint-Omer en 1783 in collaboration with John R Gwyther of the Nelson Society)

20 Corelli BARNETT : Bonaparte Page 96 – 98 Printed by George Allen & Unwin , London 1978. ISBN 0 04 944011 X

21 Robert LAFFONT: De Bonaparte à Napoléon 1798 – 1806 Page 79 ISBN 2 221 – 504 46 – 1 Librairie Plon 1972.

22 L'Arrondissement de Saint-Omer 1924 Page 99 from the notes of Captain VARLOUD du C.R.I.R.P .

23 L'Arrondissement de Saint-Omer 1924 Pg 101 Printer: L Loïez, Saint-Omer

24 L'Arrondissement de Saint-Omer 1924 Printer: L Loïez, Saint-Omer

25 Maurice BARING: Flying Corps Headquarters Page 53 Bell and Sons, London 1920.

26 L'Indépendant Newspaper Wednesday 18th November 1914

27 Quote taken from Sir Frederick Sykes and the Air Revolution 1912 – 1914 by Eric Ash Page 59

28 Taken from John Aidan Liddell the St Omer VC by Peter Daybell

29 Dan McCAFFREY Billy Bishop: Canadian Hero. Toronto: James Lorimer & Company Publishers, 1988. ISBN 1-555028-095-3. – Page 22

30 Ira JONES: King of Air Fighters, pp 65-67, Thackwell, 1934 and referred to by Peter DYE in Cross & Cockade International Journal Vol.35 No 2 2004 pg 72

31 Richard HOLMES: Fatal Avenue pg 272 Vintage Books, London 2008 ISBN 9781844139385

32 The Daily Telegraph: Britain at War Published: 1:57PM BST 21 Oct 2008

33 Auberon WAUGH Quoted from Will This Do? page 29 Random Century Ltd ISBN 0-7126-3733-8

34 Raymond DUFAY : La vie dans l'Audomarois sous L'Occupation Page 353 Les Sites de lancement de V1 dans l'Audomarois Chapter by Laurent BAILLEUL

35 Raymond DUFAY : La Vie dans l'Audomarois Sous l'Occupation pp 173 – 184.

BIBLIOGRAPHY

BARLOW Frank Thomas Becket Ed 3 Orion 1997 ISBN 1857999665 / 9781857999662

BARRY, Patrick The Penal Laws (taken from L'Osservatore Romano 30 Nov 1987)

BETHOUART M St Omer Enjeux Stratégiques de la Grande Guerre 45568 86 DS Juin 2002

BIRD Angela What to see and do in Northern France. ISBN-13:978-0-9545803-1-5

CHADWICK Hubert (SJ) St Omers to Stonyhurst Printed by Burns and Oates 1962

CHAMBERS Dictionary of World History

CLARK Alan, The Donkeys

COMITE d'HISTOIRE DU HAUT PAYS Mémoires de Guerre du Pas-de-Calais XXème Siècle Tome 17 – Année 2005 et Tome 10 (1998)

COOLEN George : La Morinie Ancienne édition by Hôtel de l'Ancien Bailliage, 42 bis Place Foch Saint-Omer

DAYBELL Peter With a Smile and a Wave : The Life of Captain Aidan Liddell VC MC. Pen and Sword Books Ltd. ISBN 1 84415 16 0 3

DERCOURT Serge Un Patrimoine Dispersé Société Académique des antiquaires de la Morinie Saint-Omer 2006

DERIEUX Philippe   Travaux et Etudes Généalogiques G.G.R.N Bourgeois de Saint Omer   1453 – 1699 recueil no: 44

DERVILLE Alain, M. Le Maner, Y Le Maner, P.Bruyelle, J. Thiébaut : Histoire de Saint-Omer Presses de Lille ISBN 2-8593-185-1

DUBARRAL Christophe St Omer dans la première Guerre Mondiale 2000 - 2001

DUCROCQ Monique La Cathédrale de Saint-Omer

DUFAY Raymond 1940 – 1944 La Vie dans L'Audomarois sous L'Occupation 1990 Imprimerie : L'Indépendant, Longuenesse

DYE Peter : The Royal Flying Corps & Royal Air Force at St-Omer, Cross & Cockade International Journal Vol.35 No.2 2004 ISBN 1360-9009

GILBERT Martin History of World War 1, Harper Collins Publishers 1995 ISBN 0 00 637 666 5

GILMARY SHEA John: Little Pictorial Lives of the Saints printed by Benzinger Brothers, New York 1894

GUNSTON Bill The Illustrated Dictionary of Fighting Aircraft of World War II published by Salamander Books Ltd 1988 ISBN 84065 092 3

HAMMERTON Sir John ABC of the RAF: Handbook for all Branches of the Air Force

HANSCOTTE François: Vauban et le Nord – La Ceinture de Fer Publisher : La Voix du Nord Editions ISBN : 2-84393-104-5

HOLMES Richard Fatal Avenue – revised edition 2008 published by Vantage ISBN 9781844139385

LE de LAUWEREYNS de ROOSENDAELE Text Mr BECQUEREREAU Photos: Album Artistique & Historique (Saint-Omer) 1893

LE de LAUWEREYNS de ROOSENDAELE Une Année Terrible : Jacqueline Robins 1881

LOTTIN et BUSSIERE Deux mille ans du Nord Pas de Calais tome 1 et 2 : Voix du Nord

Le MANER Martine Les Archives et Collections Régionales

Le MANER Yves La Libération du Nord Pas-de-Calais DVD

LEGER Sophie et PRUVOST Serge Mémoire en Images : Saint-Omer. Alan Sutton Publishing

LEVEL Bernard Les Façades des Maisons de Saint-Omer Vol 1 & II ISBN2-9514807-0-9 and 2-9514807-1-7 Société académique des Antiquaires de la Morinie 1999

MILAMON Stéphane Histoire de Longuenesse ISBN 978 2 7466 0787 3 nord'imprim

MORTIMER Ian The Life of Edward III Father of the English Nation published by Vintage 2008 ISBN 9780099527091

SHORES Christopher: Fighter Aces published by Hamlyn 1975 ISBN 600 302 30 X

SUMPTION Jonathan : The Hundred Year's War, Vol 1 Trial by Battle 1990 ISBN 0-57113-895-0

SUTTON Anne F The Mercery of London

THOMAS Guy Nord Pas-de-Calais 1939 – 1960

Trésor d'Or Catalogue for an exhibition from the 14th June – 30th September 1962 Bruges

TUCHMAN Barbara W A Distant Mirror: The Calamitous 14th Century Macmillan London ISBN 0 333 197 526

USEFUL ADDRESSES

ARC International

Zone Industrielle, 62510 ARQUES

Tel: 33 (0) 321 95 46 96

Open Monday – Friday 10.00am – 6.30pm

Saturday 10.00am – 7.00pm

Bibliothèque de Saint-Omer

40 rue Gambetta, 62500 SAINT-OMER

Tel: 33 (0) 321 38 35 08

Website: bibliotheque-st-omer.fr

Closed Sunday, Monday, Thursday

Blockhaus d'Eperlecques

Rue du Sart, 62910 EPERLECQUES

Tel: 33 (0) 321 88 44 22

Website: leblockhaus.com

La Coupole and Planetarium

History and Remembrance Centre

BP 284, 62505 SAINT-OMER cedex

Tel: 33 (0) 321 12 27 27

Website: lacoupole-france.com

Open all year round 9.00am – 6.00pm

Distillerie de Genièvre Persyn

19 route de Watten, 62910 HOULLE

Tel : 33 (0) 321 39 25 36

Email: genievrepersyn@orange.fr

ISNOR – tours of the Clairmarais marshes

Halte Fluviale, 3 rue du Marais

62500 CLAIRMARAIS

Tel: 33 (0) 321 39 15 15

Website: isnor.fr

Email: fluvial@isnor.fr

La Tour de L'Horloge

Rue du Château, 62340 GUINES

Tel: 33 (0) 321 19..59.00

Website: tour-horloge-guines.com

Maison du Papier Museum

Rue Bernard Chochoy, 62380 ESQUERDES

Tel : 33 (0) 321 95 45 25

Musée de l'hôtel Sandelin

14 rue Carnot, 62500 SAINT-OMER

Tel: 33 (0) 321 38 00 94

Email: musees-accueil@ville-saint-omer.fr

Website: ville-saint-omer.fr

Open: Wednesday – Sunday 10.00 – 12.00, 2.00pm – 6.00pm

Romelaëre Nature Park

Rue du Romelaëre, 62500 CLAIRMARAIS

Tel : 33 (0) 321 38 52 95

Website: relais-romelaere.com Closed from 15 November until 01 March

Saint-Omer Tourist Office

4 rue du Lion D'Or, 62500 SAINT-OMER

Tel: 33 (0) 321 98 08 51

Website: tourisme-saintomer.com

Email: contact@tourisme-saintomer.com

For general information about the town please visit www.ville-saint-omer.fr

REFERENCE SECTION

There are many places to stay to suit all budgets and taste in the area and you can obtain a full list from the following website: tourisme-saint-omer.com however here are some brief details to get you going.

HOTELS in Saint-Omer

ETAP Hotel * Avenue Charles de Gaulle, 62500 Saint-Omer. Close to the City Centre with ample parking, this clean and no-frills hotel is about a ten minute walk to the main square. Ideally situated for visits to the wonderful *Jardin Public* so if you have energetic children its ideal. Close also to the stair access to the Cathedral Enclos. To book online visit *etaphotel.com* or email: *h5919@accor.com* Number of rooms: 75

L'Indus Hotel ** 22 rue Louis Martel, 62500 Saint-Omer. Smack in the centre of town located in a pedestrianised part of the town very close to the main square. This hotel/restaurant has recently been completely refurbished and has been tastefully furnished. Ideally situated to access all the central attractions including the Cathedral, Musée de l'hôtel Sandelin, shops and restaurants. Be warned there is an excellent Saturday market which takes place on Place Foch every Saturday but this is usually clear by 13h00 hours. The Hotel boasts a fine seafood menu with fish delivered daily from the famous fishing port of Etaples. To book online visit *lindus.fr* or call 00 44 321 11 51 35 Number of rooms: 7

Chic O'Rail ** Place du 8 mai 1945, 62500 Saint-Omer. If you are arriving by train it couldn't be more convenient. And if hiring a car Hertz is just around the corner. The Hotel is situated just off the cobbled square in front of the majestic station built in 1905.

There are three ways into town the first being via the impressive Ruins of St Bertin abbey and from then on proceeding along the old Pilgrim Route of rue St Bertin. The second way is to walk along the Canal or Quai du Commerce and then take a left at the roundabout and proceed up the main shopping street: rue de Dunkerque. If you are curious about auctions this route will take you past the Hôtel des Ventes (Auction House) which is open Tuesday to Saturday with sale days on Mondays. The third route takes you past the War Memorial and past the old barracks which during the First World War was home to many of the British Regiments. Proceed up past Le Bretagne hotel, straight past La Poste and straight up the wide and majestic Rue Carnot. Look out on your right to see the Musée de l'hôtel Sandelin, shortly after this you will arrive at Place Victor Hugo. All three routes from the hotel to the town centre (Place Foch) take about 15 minutes. To book online visit *chicorail.fr* email: *contact@chicorail.fr* or call 00 33 321 93 59 98 Number of Rooms: 11

Les Frangins ** 5 rue Carnot, 62500 Saint-Omer. Centre of town location with a terrace onto Place Victor Hugo. It is well placed for access to Place Foch for the Saturday market, The Jardin Public, Cathedral, Musée de l'hôtel Sandelin, restaurants and shops. Parking is free for hotel residents. This hotel is part of Logis de France and has a bar and restaurant. To book online visit *frangins.fr* or email *frangins@frangins.fr* or call 00 33 321 38 12 47 Number of rooms: 26

Hotel IBIS ** 2/4 rue Henri Dupuis, 62500 Saint-Omer Situated in the heart of the town and within earshot of the peel of bells ringing out 'Immaculate Mary' this 65 room hotel has parking at the rear. Ideally placed for the town centre, Saturday market, Cathedral, Musée de l'hôtel Sandelin and the Jardin Public. The hotel also has a restaurant. To book online visit: *ibishotel.com* or email: *h0723@accor.com* or call 33 321 93 11 11

Hôtel le Saint-Louis ** 25 rue d'Arras, 62500 Saint-Omer This is another centrally located hotel with 30 bedrooms, a restaurant 'Gastronomique': Le Flaubert and an enclosed garden featuring a period red K2 Phonebox designed by Sir Giles Gilbert Scott also famous for his designs on Liverpool Cathedral, Downside Abbey and Battersea Power Station. The Hotel is in rue d'Arras which appears much wider than other streets in Saint-Omer on account of it being flattened during an allied raid in World War Two. This opened the opportunity of providing this part of the town in the early 1950's the chance of enjoying a connection to the sewage system. To book online visit *hotel-saintlouis.com* or email: *contact@hotel-saintlouis.com* or call 00 33 321 38 35 21

Le Bretagne Hotel * 2 place du Vainquai, 62500 Saint-Omer One of the larger hotels in the town and located near the railway station. Only a ten minute walk from the main square with the Saturday Market. This hotel is ideally suited for a stroll through the gardens of the ruins of l'Abbaye Saint-Bertin and if one wanted to obtain a hearty appetite it is within striking distance of the Haut Pont part of the town with its long canal and little waterways. This hotel has a restaurant. To book online visit: *hotellebretagne.com* or email: *acceuil@hotellebretagne.com* or call 00 33 321 38 25 78 Number of rooms: 69

Chambres d'Hôtes des Caps et Marais d'Opale, Quai du Commerce, 62500 Saint-Omer A typical Maison de Maitre, equivalent to a fine townhouse belonging to someone of stature. This friendly establishment is very popular and offers a wide range of activities for guests. To book online visit: *chambresdhotes.com* Tel: 00 33 321 93 89 82 email: *Bruno.hautefeuille@gmail.com*

Some hotels around Saint-Omer

Le Relais du Romelaëre * Chemin du Grand Saint-Bernard, 62500 Clairmarais. Situated right in the heart of the beautiful marshes of Clairmarais. For further information visit *relais-romelaere.com* or email *contact@relais-romelaere* or call 00 33 321 38 95 95 Number of rooms 10

Le Saint-Sébastien * 2 Place de la Libération, 62575 Blendecques. Located in the centre of this small pretty town 2 miles from Saint-Omer. To book online visit *loisirs-*

gourmets.com or email *saint-sebastien@wanadoo.fr* or call 00 33 321 38.13.05 Number of rooms 7

La Sapinière ** 12 route de Setques, 62219 Wisques. Located in the pretty village of Wisques with its famous Abbeys and monastic communities. To book online visit *sapiniere.net* or email *lasapiniere2@wanadoo.fr* or call 00 33 321 38 94 00 Number of rooms 29

La Grande Sainte-Catherine ** 51 rue Adrien Danvers, 62510 Arques. Located in the centre near to the park. For further information visit *lagrandesaintecatherine.fr* or email *alagrandesaintecatherine@orange.fr* or call 00 33 321 38 03 73 Number of rooms 8

Hôtel Golf AA *** Chemin des Bois, 62380 Acquin Westbécourt. As its name clearly implies this hotel is attached to the highly regarded 9 and 18 hole golf courses and it of course plays host to the Saint-Omer Golf Open championship every year. Many of its 54 rooms have views over the course and beyond. For further information visit *stomer-hoteldugolf.com* or email *aagolf.hotel@najeti.com* or call 00 33 321 11 42 42

Hôtel Le Moulin de Mombreux *** Chemin de Mombreux 62380 Lumbres. Well within the proximity of the Golf Aa this hotel as the name suggests is a former mill and now has been developed to a very high standard into one of the more sought-after hotels in the area. For further information visit *moulindemombreux.com* or email *contact@moulindemombreux.com* or call 00 33 321 39 13 13 Number of rooms 24

Hôtel Château Tilques **** rue du Château 62500 Tilques. Situated 3 miles out of Saint-Omer this elegant 19th Century country house is approached through the attractive little village of Tilques. The Château has tennis courts and large landscaped gardens. There is a gourmet restaurant: Le Vert Mesnil. For information online visit *chateautilques.com* or email *château-tilques.hotel@najeti.com* or call 00 33 321 88 99 99 Number of rooms 53

Hôtel Le Château de Cocove **** Avenue de Cocove, 62890 Recques-sur-Hem. Built in 1741 by Becquet de Cocove this fine building and parkland remains very popular. It also has a restaurant of note. For further information visit *chateaudecocove.com* or email *info@chateaudecocove.com* or call 00 33 321 82 68 29 Number of rooms 22

Hostellerie des 3 Mousquetaires * ** Château du Fort de la Redoute 62120 Aire-sur-la-Lys. A fine hotel with an experience of fine dining close to the historical town of Aire-sur-la-Lys. For further information visit *hostellerides3mousquetaires.com* or email *hotel.mousquetaires@wanadoo.fr* or call 00 33 321 39 01 11

Châtellerie de Schoebeque, Cassel **** 32 rue du Maréchal Foch, 59670 Cassel. Located in the historic Flemish town of Cassel the hill on which the town sits is the birth place of the nursery rhythm "The Grand Old Duke of York" and when you experience 'marching to the top of the hill' you will certainly appreciate the beautiful views and want to linger before marching all the way down again. For further information on the the hotel visit schoebeque.com or email contact@schoebeque or call 00 33 328 42 42 67 Number of rooms – a discreet 15

Château de Marconne, Marconne 62140. Located close to the centre of Hesdin. This is a highly original place to stay, beautifully restored and set in its own grounds with a lake. 7 bedrooms. For further information visit *french-country-cottages.co.uk* or email *d_van_dyk@hotmail.com*

Maison Rêve, 7 rue des Fiefs, 62380 Quercamps. Situated in a beautiful rural area and close to an excellent golf course. Gîtes for 6 people and a Chambre d'hôtes in the Pays de Lumbres. For further information call: 00 33 321 11 17 08 or email: anne-marie.journeau@orange.fr or visit www.maisonreve.fr

Made in the USA
Charleston, SC
20 October 2013